Chapter One: CHICKEN FOR EVERYDAY

Napoleon's cook once bet that he could cook chicken a different way every day of the year. The cook found that this was an easy bet to win, and I can see why, having looked at the recipes in Frank's files. Chicken's versatility seems almost endless. Perdue Farms home economists have been developing chicken recipes since the early 1970s and as a result, Frank has more than 2000 chicken recipes. If only Napoleon had chosen to bet with me, I could have won even if he'd said the bet was for six years!

In this chapter, you'll find some of Frank's and my favorites for every day cooking. But there are different kinds of every day cooking, so I've divided the chapter into three sections to take care of three different every day situations.

The first section, Fast Food Chicken from Your Refrigerator, is for when you're in a hurry and want dinner on the table in the shortest possible time. None of these recipes takes more than 15 minutes, and many are ready in five. However, you will find special tricks to make the food more interesting than just heat and serve.

The second section, Perdue Plus Five, is for when you don't mind if dinner isn't ready for another hour or so, but you want your part of the preparation to be as brief as possible. The recipes in this section use only five ingredients in addition to chicken, salt, and pepper, and all of the recipes are simple to prepareathough they may take awhile to cook.

The third section, Family Favorites, is for relaxed times. When you don't mind spending some time putting together something your family will really like, try this section. FAST FOOD CHICKEN FROM YOUR

REFRIGERATOR (PHOTO: The most valuable player on the TV Football-party table might be Perdue Done It!)

Frank loves to tell people that they can pick up delicious, fast-food chicken within easy walking distanceatheir refrigerators. "When you're hungry and in a hurry," he says, "you don't need to rush across town for great chicken. You can just walk (slowly) to your refrigerator and pick up my Perdue Done It! chicken."

Although fried foods are notoriously high in fat, particularly fast food ones. Perdue Done It! is an exception. Frank flash fries the Perdue Done It! products. They are in oil for seconds only. Further, to assure the chicken is as low in saturated fat as possible, Perdue uses only polyunsaturated soybean oil.

In the recipes that follow, I've used generic nuggets, cutlets, tenders, and other fully cooked products. However, try for the Perdue Done It! if you live in the Perdue marketing area, which is the East Coast and some of the Mid Western states. The Perdue nuggets, cutlets and tenders come from white meat fillets, while some of the other brands are pressed and formed from dark meat chicken and don't have the best texture or flavor. TENDERS, AND NUGGETS Chick on a Biscuit: Split hot baked biscuits. Fill each with a breaded chicken nugget and a thin slice of ham; top with mustard. Chicken Mexicali: Top cutlets or tenders with prepared salsa and avocado slices. Chicken Parmesan: Top partially heated cutlets with spaghetti sauce and sliced mozzarella cheese; broil briefly to melt cheese. Super Caesar Salad: Quarter heated nuggets and toss with croutons, Romaine lettuce, and Caesar salad dressing. Holiday Crepe: Heat breast tenders and place on a warm crepe. Top with cranberry sauce and roll up; serve with sour cream. Japanese Meal-in-a-Bowl: Prepare Japanese-style noodle soup (ramen) as directed. Add heated chicken breast nuggets or tenders, sliced scallions and a dash of soy sauce. (I often put this in a Thermos and bring it to Frank at his office when he's working late.) Nugget Sticks: On metal skewers, alternately thread 4 to 5 chicken breast nuggets with 2 inch pieces of bacon. Heat in oven as directed on nugget package. Dip into prepared chutney or sweet-sour sauce. Stir-Fry Snack: Stir-fry wings in a little oil with red bell pepper strips, scallions and sliced water chestnuts. Season with soy sauce. Serve over rice. Substantial Sub: Split a loaf of Italian bread lengthwise. Pile on heated breaded chicken cutlets or tenders, provolone cheese, sliced tomato, sweet onion, pimentos and shredded lettuce. Douse with bottled salad dressing and dig in. Tenders Under Wraps: Brush Boston lettuce leaves with prepared hoisin sauce or Chinese-style duck sauce. Place a heated tender or 2 nuggets and a piece of scallion on top. Roll up lettuce around tender, securing with a toothpick. PRECOOKED HOT & SPICY WINGS Chicken Antipasto: Arrange hot & spicy wings on platter with slices of provolone cheese, sliced tomatoes, marinated artichoke hearts and olives. Out-of-Buffalo Wings: Warm hot & spicy wings and arrange with celery sticks around a blue cheese dip. Combine 3/4 cup mayonnaise, 1/3 cup crumbled blue cheese and 1 minced scallion in a small bowl. Speedy Arroz Con Pollo: Prepare a box of Spanish rice mix as package directs. During last 10 minutes of cooking time, add 1 package hot & spicy wings, 1 package thawed frozen peas and 1/2 cup sliced olives. ed chicken, toasted almonds, and chopped scallions. Blend in mayonnaise flavored with curry powder and spoon back into pineapple shell to serve. Cheesy Chick: Prepare packaged stuffing mix as directed, adding 1 cup shredded Jarlsberg or Swiss cheese. Stuff whole roasted chicken or Cornish hens with mixture; heat until warmed through. Chicken Frittata: Shred roasted chicken or cut breaded chicken into cubes. Add to beaten eggs, along with mushrooms, onions, and any leftover vegetables. Cook mixture quickly, forming into an open-faced omelet or frittata. Chicken Normandy: Arrange cut-up roasted chicken or Cornish hen meat in a shallow baking dish and scatter thinly sliced apples around pieces. Cover and heat until hot and apples are tender. Stir in a little light or heavy cream and warm to serve. Chicken Reuben: Thinly slice roasted chicken. Pile on sliced rye that's been spread with Russian dressing. Top with prepared sauerkraut, a slice of Swiss cheese, and another slice of rye. Grill or pan fry sandwiches until cheese melts. Chicken Sesame: Brush roasted chicken or Cornish hens with bottled salad dressing; sprinkle surface with sesame seeds and heat as directed. Fabulous Fajitas: Slice roasted chicken into strips. Saute in oil, adding lime juice, garlic, and ground cumin to taste. Roll up in warm flour tortillas and top with chunks of avocado, chopped scallion, and cherry tomatoes. Pasta Pizazz: Saute pieces of roasted or breaded chicken with sliced zucchini, chopped onion, sliced mushrooms, and garlic. Add a dash of heavy cream and toss with hot cooked spaghetti or noodles. Power Pita: Slice roasted chicken and stuff into a whole wheat pita bread. Top with shredded carrots, alfalfa sprouts, red pepper strips and a tablespoon of dressing made of plain yogurt seasoned with lemon juice, curry powder and salt and pepper to taste. Stir Fried Chicken: Dice roasted chicken into a wok or skillet and stir-fry with scallions, celery, mushrooms, and peas. Add cooked rice and soy sauce to taste; toss well. Super Spud: Halve a baked potato and top with shredded roasted chicken mixed with a little mayonnaise. Pile on shredded Swiss cheese, bacon bits, and chopped chives; bake or microwave until cheese melts. Taco Perdue: Cube roasted chicken and serve in taco shells, topped with shredded lettuce, chopped tomatoes, onion, shredded cheese, and taco sauce. PHOTO: Harvest fruit adds seasonal flavor to chicken - 3 Golden Nugget Salad: Heat 1 package of chicken breast nuggets. Combine with Romaine lettuce, halved cherry tomatoes and diced avocado. Toss with your favorite dressing.

NUGGETS OR TENDERS WITH DIP Fully cooked breaded chicken breast nuggets (14-18 per package) or Tenders (6-8 per package) Following package directions, warm nuggets or tenders in a conventional oven or, using package tray, heat in a microwave oven. Serve with ketchup or your favorite mustard. For myself, I've been trying some of the more exotic mustards from the supermarket and sometimes I put out several kinds in pretty little dishes that I'd otherwise use for nuts. Instead of a wine or cheese tasting, my guests end up trying different mustards.

PERDUE PLUS FIVE

When was the last time you baked a pie from scratch?

I'm asking you this question because I'm guessing that you're like many other people who've told me that today they'd never have time to bake a pie from scratch. They might have once, but they don't have the time any more.

In the last few years I've asked this question to dozens and dozens of audiences when giving talks. Almost always, I get the same answer: that people who once had had the time to do a lot of cooking now seldom do. The want to eat well, they enjoy cooking, but they just can't find the time.

If you were to ask me that question, I'd have to answer that I haven't found time to bake a pie from scratch in years either. Frank keeps me so busy that sometimes I think that I'm married to a whirlwind. People joke that he's the only man you'll ever meet who can enter a revolving door in the compartment behind you and come out ahead of you. They also joke that he doesn't get ulcers$but he's a carrier.

Knowing quick recipes has become more important to me than ever, and this section contains a selection of the best. The heating and cooking time may take an hour or so, but your part in the kitchen should be no more than fifteen minutes. In this section, you'll find uncomplicated recipes with few steps, and none of the recipes have more than five ingredients in addition to chicken, salt, pepper and water.

If like me, you also are looking for ways to prepare meals that taste good, look good, give you more satisfaction than microwaving a store bought frozen dinner, but don't require a long time in the kitchen, this section is for you. BAKED ONION CHICKEN Serves 4 Recipes don't get much easier on the cook than this. Anne Nesbit developed it for Perdue Farms. One of her jobs as a Perdue home economist was to translate some of the world's most successful recipes into ones that were both easy to assemble and quick to prepare. "I'm an admirer of simple recipes," says Anne. "My heart was in this work because I believed in it. People want food that looks good and tastes good, but they don't have time to put a lot of work into getting there." I've never met Anne, except over the phone, but from this comment, I know I would like her. The recipe isn't fancy, and it may be old-fashioned, but it's a treasure when you're in a hurry. 1 chicken, cut in serving pieces dehydrated onion soup mix Preheat oven to 350oF. Roll chicken in dry soup mix, using about as much mix as you would salt. Place chicken in a single layer, skin side up, on baking sheet. Bake, uncovered for 55 to 65 minutes until cooked through. BASIC FRIED CHICKENServes 4 This is fried chicken in its simplest form. It's good enough so that the last time I made it, the grandchildren were making off with pieces almost as fast as I could cook them. Frank's daughter Anne Oliviero particularly recommends basic fried chicken served cold the next day for picnics. She and her family love to explore some of the islands off the coast of Maine, where they live, and cold fried chicken is just about always on the menu. 1/3 cup flour 1 teaspoon salt or to taste 1/4 teaspoon ground pepper or to taste 1 chicken cut in serving pieces 1/2 cup vegetable shortening In a large plastic bag combine flour with salt and pepper. Shake chicken in bag with mixture. In a large, deep skillet over medium heat, melt shortening. Cook chicken uncovered, heat for 20 to 30 minutes on each side or until cooked through. OVEN-FRIED CHICKEN, SOUTHWESTERN STYLE Any basic fried chicken recipe may be adapted for oven frying. It is a useful technique when cooking larger quantities of chicken and is less messy than stovetop frying. (Especially if you have a self-cleaning oven.) Simply follow the basic cooking instructions as given in the Southwestern version below. 1 chicken, cut in serving pieces 1 cup buttermilk 3/4 teaspoon Tabasco, optional Vegetable oil for frying 1/2 cup flour 1/2 cup corn meal 1 teaspoon salt 3/4 teaspoon chili powder 1/4 teaspoon ground pepper Place chicken in a large bowl. Sprinkle with Tabasco. Pour buttermilk over all and allow to marinate for 10 to 15 minutes. Preheat oven to 425oF. Place 1/2 inch of oil in the bottom of a heavy baking pan large enough to hold chicken without crowding. Place pan in oven to heat for 10 minutes. In a plastic bag combine remaining ingredients. Shake chicken in seasoned flour. Remove pieces one at a time and quickly slip into hot oil. Place in oven and bake for 20 minutes. Turn and bake for 10 to 15 minutes longer or until chicken is cooked through. Drain chicken on crumpled paper towels. BASIC ROAST CHICKENServes 4 Sometimes there is nothing else that will fill the bill like roasted chicken. Here's the easiest way to do it. You can brush the surface with melted butter, margarine or oil, but it isn't really necessary. 1 whole chicken 1 teaspoon salt or to taste 1 package (7-1/2-ounces) stuffing mix, prepared as directed on package Sprinkle cavity of chicken with salt. Stuff with favorite prepared stuffing. Or skip stuffing if you're really in a hurry. Place chicken in baking pan (no rack needed). ROASTING CHART

Approximate Additional Cooking

Cooking Time Amount of Time if Stuffed time

at 350F Stuffing if Stuffed Broiler/Fryer 1-1/4 to 2 hours 1-1/2 to 2 cups 15 to 20 minutes (2-1/2 to 4 pounds) Oven Stuffer Roaster 2-1/4 to 2-3/4 hours 3 to 3- 1/2 cups 20 to 25 minutes (5 to 7 pounds) Cornish Game Hen 60 to 75 minutes 1/2 to 3/4 cup 15 to 20 minutes (18-24-ounces)

BIRD OF PARADISEServes 4 The recipe calls for a chicken cut in serving pieces, but naturally you can substitute any parts that you particularly like, such as breasts or thighs. Three breasts or 6 thighs with drumsticks attached would come out to about the same amount as the 1 chicken called for in this recipe. 1 chicken, cut in serving pieces Salt and ground pepper to taste 1 egg, beaten 1/4 cup milk 1 teaspoon salt or to taste 1/3 cup grated Parmesan cheese 1/2 cup butter or margarine 1 cup sherry Season chicken with salt and pepper. In a shallow bowl combine egg and milk. Place cheese in a shallow baking pan. Dip chicken in egg mixture; then roll in cheese. In a large, deep skillet, over medium heat, melt butter. Add chicken and brown for 5 to 6 minutes on each side. Add sherry. Cover and cook at medium-low heat for 35 to 45 minutes or until cooked through. CORN CRISPED CHICKENServes 4 I grew up on this recipe. It's not new, but it's good and the preparation time is minimal. If you don't have cornflakes, you can substitute almost any breakfast flakes as long as they don't have raisins in them. (The raisins can scorch in the oven.) For variation, you can add 1 teaspoon dried italian seasonings or 1 teaspoon chili powder or 3/4 teaspoon curry powder to the cornflake crumbs. 1 cup cornflake crumbs 1 teaspoon salt or to taste 1/4 teaspoon ground pepper 1/2 cup evaporated milk, undiluted 1 chicken, cut in serving pieces Preheat oven to 350oF. On a sheet of wax paper combine cornflake crumbs, salt and pepper. Place evaporated milk in a shallow bowl. Dip chicken in milk; then roll in seasoned crumbs. Place chicken, skin side up, in a baking pan. Bake, uncovered for 1 hour, or until cooked through.

CUTLET PAILLARDS WITH BASIL BUTTER Serves 4 When I made this recipe, I happened to be in a hurry, and didn't have time to get fresh basil so I used dried basil instead. Frank liked it and had seconds. The name "Paillard," by the way, comes from a European restaurant famous at the end of the 19th Century. 4 skinless, boneless chicken breast halves or 1 thin sliced boneless roaster breast 1 tablespoon olive or vegetable oil 6 tablespoons butter or margarine 3 tablespoons minced fresh basil, or 1 tablespoon dried 1 small clove garlic, minced 1 teaspoon lemon juice salt and ground pepper to taste lemon slices, for garnish Place chicken between sheets of plastic wrap and pound to 1/2 inch thickness. If using thin sliced boneless Roaster breast, omit placing in plastic wrap and pounding. Brush cutlets lightly with oil, Grill over hot coals 3 to 4 minutes per side, rotating to form crosshatch marks characteristic of paillards, or broil 3 to 4 minutes per side or until cooked through. Place butter, basil, garlic and lemon juice in a small pan and melt on the side of the grill. Spoon butter over paillards and season with salt and pepper. Garnish with lemon slices. EASY OVEN CHICKEN Serves 4 This recipe has been one of my favorites since college days. The true chicken flavor comes out with just a touch of garlic. 1 chicken, cut in serving pieces 1/4 cup olive or vegetable oil 1 teaspoon salt or to taste 1/4 teaspoon ground pepper 1 small clove garlic, minced Preheat oven to 350oF. In a shallow baking pan arrange chicken in a single layer, skin side up. Pour oil over chicken. Sprinkle with salt, pepper and garlic. Bake, uncovered, for about 1 hour, or until cooked through.

HONEY LEMON CHICKEN Serves 4 This recipe was originally designed for broiling, but this version requires less attention. 1 chicken, cut in serving pieces 1/2 cup honey 1/4 cup lemon juice 1 teaspoon salt or to taste Preheat oven to 350oF. In a shallow baking pan arrange chicken in a single layer, skin side down. In a small bowl combine honey, lemon juice and salt. Pour half of this sauce over chicken. Bake, covered for 30 minutes. Remove cover; turn chicken. Pour other half of sauce on chicken. Replace cover. Bake another 25 to 30 minutes or until cooked through, removing cover last 10 minutes for browning. HONEY-MUSTARD BAKED BREASTServes 4 Have you ever been concerned about whether the honey you have in your cupboard is fresh or whether it should be thrown out? Not to worry! Honey is itself a natural preservative and samples of honey have been found in the tombs of Ancient Egypt that were still edible. If it's crystallized, it may look bad, but it's still a wholesome food. Just heat it gently until it reliquifies. 1 whole boneless roaster breast salt and ground pepper to taste 4 tablespoons melted butter or margarine 1/2 cup honey 1/4 cup Dijon mustard 1/4 teaspoon curry powder Preheat oven to 350oF. Season breast with salt and pepper. Combine butter, honey, mustard and curry powder. Spoon half of sauce into a shallow baking dish. Add breast and turn to coat well. Bake, uncovered, for about 1 hour or until cooked through. Turn and baste with remaining sauce once during cooking time.

IT'S A DILLY CHICKEN When I read this recipe in the files, I noticed several hand-scrawled notes saying that it was really good, and someone described it as "a dilly of a recipe." Yet from reading the recipe, it didn't sound as special as the notes indicated, especially since the ingredients include canned mushrooms rather than fresh. I was curious enough that I went to the kitchen and made the recipe, expecting that this would be one of the recipes that I wouldn't include in this book. But to my surprise, I discovered that yes, dill seed and canned mushrooms, along with the juice from the mushrooms, really do something terrific for chicken. It's not rich or creamy, but there's an attractive, aromatic flavor that permeates the chicken. 1 chicken, cut in serving pieces 1 teaspoon salt or to taste 1/4 teaspoon ground pepper 1 can (4-ounces) whole small mushrooms (with liquid) 1/2 teaspoon dill seed Preheat oven to 350oF. In a shallow baking pan arrange chicken, skin side up, in a single layer. Add salt, pepper, mushrooms (with liquid from can) and dill. Cover with foil. Bake at for 1 hour or until cooked through.

KIWI GLAZED CORNISH HENS Serves 2 Kiwifruit is only sweet and mild when it's fully ripe. A kiwifruit grower told me that kiwifruits are ripe when they're "soft as a baby's bottom." When they're underripe, they taste like something between a lemon and a crabapple. If your kiwifruit is hard when you bring it home, give it a couple of days to ripen on your kitchen counter. 2 fresh Cornish game hens salt and ground pepper to taste 3 tablespoons butter or margarine 1 tablespoon sugar 1 ripe kiwifruit, peeled and mashed Preheat oven to 350oF. Remove giblets. Season hens inside and out with salt and pepper. Tie legs together, fold wings back and arrange in baking pan. In a small saucepan over medium-low heat, melt butter. Brush hens with 2 tablespoons butter, reserving remainder. Put hens in oven, and while they are cooking, prepare kiwi glaze. Add sugar to remaining butter in pan and heat over medium-low until sugar dissolves. Add mashed kiwi and cook one minute. Remove from heat. After 45 minutes of cooking time, brush hens generously with kiwi glaze. Continue baking for 15 to 20 minutes or until juices run clear with no hint of pink when thigh is pierced.

FAMILY FAVORITES In contrast to the preceding recipes, these recipes have more ingredients and require more preparation time, but if you've got the time, they're worth it. If you want to minimize time in the kitchen using these recipes, here are some suggestions. Tips for Saving Time in the Kitchen

_To halve baking time, select boneless chicken breasts. Cooking time is only 15-20 minutes at 350oF. A bone-in breast takes 35-45 minutes.

_Stir fry chicken can be done in as little as 4 minutes.

_Cook double batches and freeze the extras in serving size packages. On days when time is short, pop a package into the microwave for "fast food."

_Take advantage of your supermarket's time-saving convenience items. If you're in a hurry, don't bother to slice and chop your fresh ingredients. The salad bar has probably done it for you. You can also find time savers such as shredded cheese and frozen chopped onion. (The supermarket industry has watched restaurants and fast food stores take more and more of your food dollars away each year. They're now doing everything they can think of to reverse this trend and make supermarket shopping so attractive, quick, convenient and economical that you'll want to cook at home.)

_Learn to cook chicken in the microwave. A pound of broiler parts that would take 40 minutes in a 350 degree oven takes only 6-10 minutes in the microwave. See Chapter Four, Chicken in the Microwave.

SOUPS

PHOTO: Pot of soup with fresh vegetables surrounding outside - 2

Wherever there are people and chickens, there are chicken soups. Virtually every immigrant group arriving in America brought along favorite chicken soup recipes and often the treasured family soup pot, too.

If you grew up on canned, frozen, and dried soups, you may not realize how easy it is to make truly wonderful soups at home. If so, try it for yourself, perhaps with these American classics. All the soups are based on a key ingredient: rich, homemade chicken stock, made from either whole birds or from parts, in about three hours. Stock takes little tending, just slow easy cooking to bring out all the flavor and wholesome goodness. Why not try making one of these soups now? And then, with the help of your freezer, enjoy the results many times in the coming months. Basic Guide to Chicken Soup

_Older, larger birds, such as the 5-7 pound roasters, make the best soups. An older bird will have developed more of the rich, intense chickeny flavor than the younger, milder-flavored broilers or Cornish hens. I've made soup from broilers and while it wasn't bad, it wasn't as good as it could be.

_Use roaster parts if you want to save time. They cook faster and are excellent when you need only a small amount of broth. The richest flavor, by the way, comes from the muscles that are exercised most, which happen to be the dark meat muscles. All parts will make satisfactory soup, but the legs, thighs and necks provide the fullest flavor.

_For clear, golden broth, do not add liver. It turns stock cloudy. And avoid a greenish cast by using only parsley stems and the white parts of leeks or scallions.

_As the stock cooks down, foam will float to the top. Skim it off, or strain it out through double cheesecloth when the stock is complete. Tie herbs and greens in cheesecloth as a "bouquet garni," so you won't inadvertently remove them during the skimming.

_Always simmer stock over low to medium heat. It's not a good idea to boil the stock for the same reason it's not a good idea to boil coffee; too much of the flavor would boil away into the air. _Leftover vegetables and those past their prime are good pureed in cream soups. When thickening such recipes with egg, prevent curdling by stirring a cup of hot soup first into egg, then back into soup. Also, be careful to keep the soup from boiling once you've added the egg.

_Most soups develop better flavor if you'll store them, covered, in the refrigerator for a day or two. To seal in the flavor while you're storing the soup, don't remove the fat that's on top. When you're ready to serve the soup you can lift the congealed fat off as a sheet. To remove the last particles of fat, place unscented paper towel on the surface. Draw towel to one side and remove.

_When freezing stock, allow 1/2- to 1-inch head room in containers so soup can expand. Freeze some in quart- sized or larger containers for use in soups. Ladle the rest into ice cube trays or muffin cups for adding to vegetables, sauces, or gravies. Freeze and then transfer frozen stock cubes to a plastic bag or freezer container and keep frozen until ready to use.

_Soup may be stored in the refrigerator two or three days or frozen for three to four months. When reheating, make sure to bring the broth to a boil. Soups enriched with eggs are, unfortunately, not good candidates for reheating; they're apt to curdle. BASIC CHICKEN STOCK Makes about 8 cups If you need to, you can make the following substitutions for the roaster: 1 stewing hen or spent fowl (5-7 pounds); 2 fresh young chickens (2-4 pounds); or 6 pounds fresh chicken parts, preferably dark meat portions. (As I mentioned earlier, young chickens will not provide as rich a flavor as the older birds but the taste will still be good.) Cooking times for meat will vary from 3 hours for stewing hens or spent fowl, to 1-1/2 hours for 2 smaller birds to slightly less time for parts. In each case, time from beginning of simmer and return bones to stock for an additional 1/2 hour after you've removed the meat. Chicken stock is delicious served as a simple broth with herbs, shredded or julienne vegetables, slivers of meat, or rice. It also is the base from which countless other soups are made. 1 roaster (5-7 pounds) chicken giblets, except liver 1 large bay leaf 2 whole cloves 1 teaspoon white peppercorns 1 1/2 teaspoons fresh thyme or 1/2 teaspoon dried 4 quarts water or enough to cover chicken generously 1 cup dry white wine, optional 2 medium onions, quartered 2 large carrots, sliced 2 ribs celery, sliced 1 leek, white part only, cleaned and sliced, optional 1 bunch fresh parsley, stems only 1 teaspoon salt or to taste Remove giblets from roaster and discard bird-watcher thermometer, if it has one. Place roaster along with giblets in a large stockpot (8 to 10 quarts) or other large sauce pot. Wrap bay leaf, cloves, peppercorns, and thyme in cheesecloth as bouquet garni; tie closed with string. Add to stockpot along with remaining ingredients. Cover pot and simmer over medium-low heat for 2-1/2 hours or until meat is tender. Carefully skim stock from time to time with a ladle or spoon to remove fat particles and foam. To check roaster for doneness, pull back a leg or cut into meat close to bone; it is cooked when no pink color remains in meat. Remove pieces with a slotted spoon. Cut away meat from bones and return bones to stock; simmer 30 minutes longer. (See Chapter 10: Cooking with Leftovers for uses for the cooked meat.) Strain stock through a fine sieve. If you want, prepare in advance to this point and refrigerate or freeze. Skim off top fat before using. To make a soup, bring as much stock as needed to a simmer. Then follow the soup recipe, adding chicken, vegetables, thickeners, seasonings, and garnishes. CHICKEN-IN-EVERY-POT SOUPServes 4-6 For the best flavor, use fresh vegetables, varying them according to the season. Speaking of fresh vegetables, do you know how to tell a good carrot? Look at the "crown," (that's the stem end). If the crown is turning brown or black or has regrowth visible where the stem was, you've got a carrot that's been around awhile. If the crown and shoulders are a bright orange, you've got a nice, fresh carrot. 1 cup potatoes, cut in 1/2-inch cubes 4 cups chicken broth 1/4 cup dry sherry 1 teaspoon salt or to taste 1/8 teaspoon ground pepper 1 cup onions, halved and thinly sliced 1 cup carrots, in 1/4-inch by 2-inch sticks 1 cup celery, in 1/4-inch by 2-inch sticks 1 cup fresh or frozen green beans, in 2-inch pieces 2 cups cooked chicken, in 1/4-inch by 2-inch julienne strips 1 cup zucchini, in 1/4-inch by 2-inch sticks Place potatoes in a saucepan with enough salted water to cover. Bring to a boil over medium-high heat. Cook potatoes 5 minutes; drain, rinse under cold water and set aside. In large saucepan over medium-high heat, bring broth and sherry to a boil. Season with salt and pepper. Add onions, carrots, and celery and simmer 5 minutes. Stir in green beans and chicken and heat soup to boiling. Add zucchini and potatoes and simmer 1 minute longer or until vegetables are as tender as you like them. Variation: Chicken Minestrone Add 1 cup chopped stewed tomatoes in their juice and 2 cups cooked, drained fusilli or other pasta and 1/2-cup cooked kidney beans when adding zucchini and potatoes. Stir in 1/2-cup grated Parmesan cheese just before serving. Other fresh vegetables may be added according to their cooking times. Minestrone happens to be one of Frank's favorites, although he skips the cheese because of its cholesterol. NEW ENGLAND CHICKEN 'N' CORN CHOWDERServes 4-6 Chowders are thick soups which take their name from the large French pot used in soup-making called a "chaudiere." You can use fresh corn in this recipe, but I deliberately suggested frozen corn first because frozen corn can actually taste sweeter and fresher than the fresh corn you buy at the supermarket. Corn loses 50% of its sweetness in just 24 hours at room temperature, and it can take days for corn to get from the fields to the supermarket to your house. In contrast, frozen corn is rushed from the fields to the freezer in just a few hours, and once frozen, it stops losing its sweetness. Strange as it may seem, with corn, frozen can taste fresher than fresh. 1/4 pound bacon or salt pork, diced 1 cup chopped onion 1/2 cup chopped celery 4 cups chicken broth 2 cups peeled potatoes, cut in 1/2-inch cubes 1 package (10 ounces) frozen corn or kernels from 2 ears of corn 1 teaspoon salt or to taste 1/8 teaspoon ground pepper 2 cups cooked, diced chicken 1 cup (1/2-pint) heavy cream Oyster crackers, for garnish In large saucepan over medium-high heat, saute bacon for 3 minutes until its fat has been rendered. Add onions and celery and cook 3 minutes longer. Stir in broth and bring to a boil, whisking constantly. Add potatoes and corn, season with salt and pepper and cook 5 to 10 minutes or until tender. Stir in chicken and cream, simmer 3 minutes and serve with oyster crackers. Variation: Shellfish Chowder Add 1 cup chopped green pepper and 1 cup cooked crab or shrimp to soup when adding chicken.

HEARTY LANCASTER CHICKEN, VEGETABLE AND DUMPLING SOUP Serves 4 This is a famous Pennsylvania summer soup made with extra vegetables for hearty winter eating. You can substitute noodles for the dumplings, or add crackers, pretzels $ and some people have told me that even popcorn works. I'm skeptical about the popcorn, but if you're feeling adventurous, give it a try. 6 cups chicken broth 2 cups cooked, diced chicken 1 teaspoon salt or to taste 1/8 teaspoon ground pepper 1/2 cup parboiled potatoes, cut in 1/2-inch cubes 1/2 cup parboiled carrots, cut in 1/2-inch pieces 1/2 cup shredded green cabbage 1 cup thinly-sliced leek, white and tender green parts only, or 1 medium onion, thinly sliced 1 package (10-ounces) frozen corn kernels from 2 ears of corn Knepp In large saucepan over high heat, bring broth to a boil. Add other ingredients and reduce heat to low. Simmer for 3 minutes while making dumplings. Knepp (Little Dumplings) 1 egg 3/4 cup flour 1/3 cup water 1/4 teaspoon salt or to taste 1/8 teaspoon baking powder Pinch ground nutmeg 1 teaspoon minced, fresh parsley, optional garnish In small bowl, beat egg; stir in flour, water, salt, baking powder, and nutmeg. Drop batter by half teaspoons into the simmering soup. When dumplings rise to top, stir in parsley and serve. Variation: Chicken Spinach Straciatella Omit dumplings. Clean and stem 1/2 pound fresh spinach; stack and cut into 1/2-inch strips. Whisk together 2 eggs with 1/2-cup grated Parmesan cheese. Stir in spinach with chicken, then heat soup just to boiling. Immediately pour in the egg mixture in a thin stream, while stirring. The goal is to end up with thread-like strands of cooked egg. Cook until soup simmers again; stir gently just before serving.

STEW FROM BAVARIAServes 4 If you like mild sauerkraut, instead of just draining it, as the recipe suggests, rinse it in a colander or strainer. 1 roaster boneless breast, cut into bite-size pieces salt and ground pepper to taste 2 tablespoons butter or margarine 1 medium onion, thinly sliced 1 pound sauerkraut, drained 1 can (16 ounces) whole berry cranberry sauce 1 large apple, peeled, cored and sliced 1/2 cup chopped walnuts (optional)

Season breast pieces with salt and pepper. In a flame proof casserole or Dutch oven over medium heat, melt butter. Add chicken and onions. Saute until lightly browned, about 5 minutes. In a bowl combine sauerkraut, cranberry sauce and apples. Spoon over chicken and onions and toss gently. Cover and simmer over medium-low heat for 20 minutes. Sprinkle with walnuts just before serving.

MAIN DISH RECIPES RECIPES WITH CHICKEN BREASTS Unlike women, chickens have only one breast. A single serving would usually be a breast half. The recipes that follow will refer to "breasts" and "breast halves." A cutlet is a breast half (or thigh) that is both skinless and boneless and sometimes has been pounded to flatten. A scaloppine is a cutlet sliced almost in half lengthwise and then opened, like the wings of a butterfly or a thin slice from a large roaster breast. To save time, look for chicken scaloppine which have already been made for you: the Perdue thin-sliced Oven Stuffer Roaster Breasts are ready-made scaloppine.

The recipes will also specify whether to use a chicken breast or a roaster breast. You can interchange them, but the results will be different. A roaster has a more intense flavor and is juicier. It's also bigger, and requires longer cooking. BAKED BREASTS WITH CHEESEServes 4 When the Perdue Oven Stuffer Roasters and Roaster Parts first came out, Frank used to have recipe cards put in each one because it was a new product and most people didn't know how they should be cooked. The practice was discontinued once Roasters became well-known. The woman in charge of distributing recipes told me that sometimes the recipes on the cards became family favorites, and when a person lost one of the family favorite cards, he or she would actually take the trouble to write to Frank for a replacement. I asked how often this happens and learned that over the years, Frank has received thousands of letters requesting replacement cards. This is one of the recipes that people have asked for over and over again. 3 tablespoons butter or margarine, divided 1 roaster boneless breast salt and ground pepper to taste 2 scallions, thinly sliced 1 tablespoon fresh chopped parsley 1 and 1/2 teaspoons fresh thyme or 1/2 teaspoon dried 1/2 cup chicken broth 3 tablespoons dry white wine 3/4 cup grated Swiss cheese 2 tablespoons grated Parmesan cheese 2 tablespoons bread crumbs Preheat oven to 375oF. Lightly butter a shallow baking dish. Place chicken in baking dish and sprinkle with salt, pepper, scallions, parsley, and thyme. In a measuring cup combine broth and wine and pour over chicken. Cover and bake 20 minutes. In a small bowl combine cheeses and bread crumbs. Remove chicken from oven and sprinkle with cheese mixture. Dot with remaining butter and place under broiler until cheese is melted and golden. BERLINER SCHNITZEL BREASTServes 4 You'll notice that the "hard-cooked" egg in this recipe isn't called "hard-boiled." The reason is that the egg producers tell me that it's better never to boil an egg, but rather to cook it until it's hard in water that's just below boiling. If you cook your eggs in boiling water, they'll end up with an unattractive greenish color where the yolk meets the white. At lower temperatures, the yolk will be more tender and won't discolor. 1 roaster boneless breast or a package of thin sliced boneless roaster breast. 2 eggs 3/4 teaspoon salt or to taste Ground pepper to taste 1/3 cup flour 1 cup dry breadcrumbs vegetable oil 6 tablespoons butter or margarine 2 tablespoons fresh lemon juice 3 tablespoons capers, drained 1 hard-cooked egg, finely chopped 2 tablespoons minced fresh parsley Separate fillets from breast halves and then cut breast halves in half, lengthwise. Place breast pieces between sheets of plastic wrap. Pound chicken to a 1/4-inch thickness to form scaloppine. If using thin sliced breast skip this step. In a shallow bowl beat eggs with salt and pepper. Place flour and bread crumbs on sheets of wax paper. Dredge chicken in flour then dip in egg and coat with breadcrumbs. Heat 1/4-inch oil in a large skillet over medium-high heat. Add chicken and saute for 3 to 4 minutes per side or until cooked through. Remove to serving platter. Pour oil from skillet and wipe clean. Add butter to skillet and melt over medium heat. Add lemon juice and capers carefully to avoid spatters; pour over schnitzels. In a small bowl toss together hard- cooked egg and parsley and sprinkle over top. Serve with buttered noodles. BONELESS BREAST PARMESANServes 4 To get the best flavor from the tomatoes, make sure your supermarket doesn't store them on the chilling shelf and don't refrigerate them when you bring them home. Store them at room temperature and use them soon after you buy them. 1 roaster boneless breast or thin sliced boneless roaster breast 1 1/4 teaspoons salt, divided Ground pepper to taste 2 eggs, beaten 3/4 cup plain bread crumbs 3/4 cup grated Parmesan cheese 1/3 cup flour 1 pound fresh ripe tomatoes, chopped 1 small clove garlic, minced 3/4 cup olive oil, divided 2 tablespoons minced fresh basil or 2 teaspoons dried Separate fillets from breast halves and then cut breast halves in half, lengthwise. Place breast pieces between sheets of plastic wrap and pound to 1/4" thickness to form scaloppine. If using thin sliced breast, skip the previous step. In a shallow bowl beat eggs with 3/4 teaspoon salt and pepper. Place flour on a sheet of wax paper. On another sheet of wax paper combine bread crumbs and Parmesan cheese. Dredge cutlets in flour, dip in egg and roll in bread crumb mixture. Refrigerate while making sauce. In a small serving bowl combine tomatoes, garlic, 1/4 cup olive oil, basil and salt and pepper. In a large skillet over medium-high heat, heat remaining oil. Add chicken and saute for 3 to 4 minutes per side or until cooked through. Transfer to a warmed serving dish. Pass sauce separately. BREAST COQ AU VIN Serves 4 The famous food writer, Malcolm R. Herbert, tells a story that I've always loved about coq au vin (chicken in wine). According to Herbert, a lady lavished praise on Alexander Dumaine, one of France's outstanding chefs, for his version of chicken in wine.

"Madam, I'm not satisfied," Dumaine replied.

"But you have been making coq au vin for 30 years," the woman protested. "How can you not be satisfied?"

"That, madam, was practice."

According to Herbert, Dumaine's version of coq au vin uses red wine, white wine, and brandy, and it takes a good twenty-four hours to prepare. This version is a lot simpler, but still very good. The day I made it, I couldn't find pearl onions or small onions in my local supermarket, so I used a large white onion, chopped. The pearl onions would have been prettier, but the taste was fine. 2 tablespoons butter or margarine 1 roaster breast 1 cup dry red wine salt and ground pepper to taste 1 sprig each of fresh thyme and rosemary or 1/4 teaspoon each, dried 1 clove garlic, minced 16 pearl onions, if available, otherwise 8 small white onions, peeled and quartered, or 1 large onion, chopped. 1/4 pound fresh mushrooms, quartered 1 tablespoon cornstarch 1/4 cup water 2 slices bacon, cooked and crumbled 1 tablespoon fresh minced parsley In a Dutch oven over medium-high heat, melt butter. Add breast and brown on all sides, 12 to 15 minutes. Add wine, seasonings, garlic and onions. Cover and simmer 60 minutes. Add mushrooms and simmer 10 to 15 minutes longer or until breast is cooked through. Drain juices into a small saucepan; blend cornstarch and water; stir into pan juices and cook, over medium heat, stirring constantly, one minute or until sauce thickens and clears. Carve breast and serve with wine sauce. Garnish with crumbled bacon and parsley.

BREAST WITH APPLE-PECAN STUFFINGServes 4 Make sure that the pecans you use are fresh. In the shell, they'll last in a cool dry place for six months. Shelled pecans should be kept in the refrigerator, in an air tight container. If you plan to keep them for longer than half a year, freeze them.

Have you ever wondered just what a "Cornish game hen" is?

It's a very young bird, usually about 5 weeks old, as opposed to a broiler, which is 7 weeks, or a roaster, which is 12 weeks. Typically, they're tenderer and slightly lower in fat than older birds.

All Cornish game hens are very young chickens, but the Perdue Cornish game hens have something else special about them. Frank directed the Perdue geneticists to breed the broadest breasted Cornish hens in the industry. Like the Perdue Roasters, the Perdue Cornish have exceptionally broad breasts. The ratio of meat to bone is therefore particularly favorable.

BUFFALO-STYLE CORNISH PIECES

Serves 2

You can re-use the frying oil called for in this recipe, or any deep frying recipe, for that matter. As long as you never heat the oil to the smoking point and as long as you strain it through cheese cloth to remove any particles of food, you can use it over and over again. The oil is still good as long as it retains it's golden color. When it has turned a dark brown, it's time to replace it. If you don't have cheese cloth handy for straining, laundered nylon stockings make a good substitute.

Creamy Blue Cheese Dressing
1/2 cup mayonnaise
1/4 cup sour cream
2 tablespoons crumbled blue cheese
2 tablespoons minced fresh parsley
1 tablespoon fresh lemon juice
1 scallion, thinly sliced
1 small clove garlic, minced
2 fresh Cornish game hens
salt and ground pepper to taste
oil for deep frying
2 tablespoons butter or margarine, melted
2 tablespoons Tabasco

In a small serving bowl prepare dressing by blending mayonnaise and sour cream. Stir in blue cheese, parsley, lemon juice, scallion and garlic. Chill. Quarter hens and remove backbones. Pat pieces dry with paper towels and season with salt and pepper. Heat oil to 375oF or until a small cube of bread sizzles when placed in oil. Deep-fry hens 10 minutes, turning once. Drain well. In a small bowl blend melted butter and hot sauce; brush on chicken pieces. Serve warm with Creamy Blue Cheese Dressing.

CORNISH SAUTE WITH SUMMER SQUASH

Serves 2

To keep the olive oil called for in this recipe in its best condition, store it in an airtight container in a cool cupboard away from the light. It's not necessary to refrigerate it, and besides cold temperatures will make it cloudy and difficult to pour.

2 fresh Cornish game hens
salt and ground pepper to taste
2 tablespoons olive oil
1 medium onion, sliced
1 clove garlic, minced
1 medium zucchini, sliced
1 medium yellow squash, sliced
1/2 cup chicken broth
2 tablespoons minced fresh parsley
1 tablespoon fresh lemon juice

Halve hens and remove backbones. Season with salt and pepper. In a large skillet, over medium-high heat, heat oil. Add hen halves and brown on all sides, 10 to 12 minutes. Add onion and garlic; saute 3 to 4 minutes. Add squash, broth, parsley and lemon juice. Cover, reduce heat to medium-low, and cook 15 to 20 minutes or until hens are cooked through.

GRECIAN HEN SAUTE

Serves 2

Do you know the easiest way to peel the fresh tomatoes called for in this recipe? Place the tomatoes in boiling water for about 20-40 seconds and you'll find that the skin slips off quite easily. The riper the tomato, the quicker the skin loosens in boiling water.

2 fresh Cornish game hens
2 tablespoons olive oil
1 clove garlic, minced
1 bay leaf
1 and 1/2 teaspoon minced, fresh oregano or 1/2 teaspoon dried
salt and ground pepper to taste
1/2 cup white wine
2 ripe tomatoes, peeled and quartered
1/4 pound feta cheese, cut into 1/2" cubes
2 tablespoons ripe olives, sliced

Cut hens into quarters and remove backbones. In a large skillet over medium-high heat, heat oil. Add chicken and brown 5 to 6 minutes per side. Add garlic, bay leaf, oregano, salt, pepper and wine. Cover and simmer over medium-low heat for 15 minutes. Add tomatoes and cook 10 minutes. Stir in cheese and olives. Cook 5 minutes longer or until hens are cooked through. Remove bay leaf before serving.

HENS NORMANDY WITH APPLES

Serves 2

If you're not using the apples in this recipe the day you buy them, store them in the refrigerator. Apples age five times faster at room temperature than they do in the refrigerator so they'll keep fresher longer if you store them in the refrigerator instead of in a fruit bowl. 2 fresh Cornish game hens salt and ground pepper to taste 1 tablespoon minced, fresh sage or 1 teaspoon dried 3 tablespoons butter or margarine, melted 2/3 cup apple juice 2 Golden Delicious apples, peeled 1/3 cup chicken broth or white wine 1/2 cup heavy cream 1 tablespoon minced fresh parsley Season hens inside and out with salt and pepper. Put 1/2 of sage in each cavity. Tie legs together and fold wings back. Place hens in a flame proof baking pan just large enough to hold them comfortably. Brush with melted butter. Add apple juice to baking pan. Bake at 350oF 30 minutes, basting several times. Core and quarter apples; add to pan and baste. Bake 30 minutes, until hens and apples are tender, basting several times. Remove hens and apples to serving platter; keep warm. On top of stove, bring pan drippings to a boil; add broth or wine and cook until reduced by half. Stir in cream; cook 2 to 3 minutes until slightly thickened. Pour sauce over hens and apples. Sprinkle with parsley and serve. WINE-COUNTRY CORNISHServes 4 When you buy (or pick) the tomatoes called for in this recipe, store them at room temperature rather than in the refrigerator. The tomato farmers say that refrigerator temperatures destroy a tomato's flavor and texture. Try to use tomatoes soon after you buy them while they're still at their best. 4 fresh Cornish game hens salt and ground pepper to taste 3 tablespoons olive oil 1 large onion, thinly sliced 2 cloves garlic, minced 1 tablespoon flour 1/2 cup dry white wine or vermouth 1/2 cup chicken broth 2 tomatoes, peeled and chopped 2 tablespoons tomato paste 1 1/2 teaspoons minced, fresh oregano or 1/2 teaspoon dried Season hens inside and out with salt and pepper. Fold wings back and tie legs together. In a Dutch oven large enough to hold all 4 Cornish, over medium-high heat, heat oil. Brown hens on breast side. If you don't have a pan big enough to do four at a time, brown one or two at a time. Remove hens and reserve. Add onion and garlic and saute for 5 minutes. Stir in flour. Add remaining ingredients and season to taste with salt and pepper. Stir. Return hens to Dutch oven breast side up, and bring liquid to a boil. Reduce heat to medium-low, cover and simmer for 45 minutes. Cornish are done when juices run clear with no hint of pink when thigh is pierced.

RECIPES WITH CHICKEN PIECES

In the early 1970s, 75% of the chicken sold was whole chicken. Today it's less than 25%. If you want to substitute all legs or all breasts or some other combination, look at the table in the Introduction, page s 12-13 for a chart showing equivalent amounts of the different parts.

BATTER FRIED CHICKEN

Serves 4

I bet you can make this in less time than it takes to drive to the local fast food place and wait in line for service and drive back again. It should cost a lot less too. Remember, you can re-use the frying oil many times. Just don't let it get so hot that it smokes and be sure to strain it after you've finished with the frying.

1-1/3 cups flour
1 teaspoon salt or to taste
1/4 teaspoon ground pepper
2 teaspoons baking powder
1 cup milk
1 egg, beaten
1 chicken cut in serving pieces
Oil for deep frying

In a mixing bowl combine dry ingredients; add milk and egg gradually to make batter. Dip chicken in batter. In a deep fryer heat oil to 350oF. Add chicken and fry for 15 to 25 minutes until cooked through.

BEER AND PRETZELS CHICKEN

Serves 4

This dish is at its best when the bacon and pretzels are finely chopped. Use your blender or food processor to make the job easy.

1/3 cup flour
1 teaspoon paprika
1 teaspoon salt or to taste
1/4 teaspoon ginger
1/4 teaspoon ground pepper
1/2 cup beer
1 egg
1/2 cup finely crushed pretzels
1/4 cup grated Parmesan cheese
2 slices bacon, cooked crisp, crumbled
3 tablespoons minced, fresh parsley
1 chicken cut in serving pieces

In a mixing bowl combine flour, paprika, salt, ginger and pepper. Add beer and egg; beat with a hand beater to make smooth batter. Mix crushed pretzels, Parmesan cheese, bacon and parsley in a large plastic bag. Dip chicken pieces one a time in batter; then place in bag with pretzel mix and shake to coat. Place coated chicken pieces in shallow baking pan, skin side up. Bake, covered, at 350oF for 30 minutes. Remove cover. Continue baking, uncovered, about 30 minutes longer or until chicken is cooked through. CAPITAL CHICKEN Serves 4 This is rather highly seasoned dish. Your family might prefer it with a little less ginger—but then again, maybe they'll love it this strong. 1 chicken, cut in serving pieces 2 teaspoons ground ginger 1/2 teaspoon dried oregano 2 tablespoons brown sugar 1 tablespoon flour 2 cloves garlic, sliced 1/2 cup rose wine 1/2 cup soy sauce 1/2 cup oil 1/4 cup water Preheat oven to 350oF. Place chicken in single layer, skin side up, in shallow baking pan. In a mixing bowl combine remaining ingredients and pour over chicken. Bake, uncovered for about 1 hour or until cooked through, basting occasionally. CHICKEN ORANGE-ANO Serves 4 When you're making this recipe, what if you find that your brown sugar has hardened into a brick and you can't measure it anymore? I used to take a hammer and wallop it and then use the pieces. But then a sugar cane producer told me that a short term emergency solution is to heat the sugar at 250 degrees in the oven until it softened. The advantage of this is that it works. The disadvantage is that whatever's left is twice as hard once it cools. You can re-heat it again, but it gets more brick-like with each heating. 1/3 cup flour 1 teaspoon salt or to taste 1/8 teaspoon ground pepper 1 chicken, cut in serving pieces 1/4 cup butter or margarine 1 can (6-ounces) frozen orange juice concentrate 1 can (6-ounces) water 2 tablespoons dark brown sugar 1/4 teaspoon dried oregano 1/2 teaspoon nutmeg In a large plastic bag, combine flour salt and pepper. Add chicken pieces and shake to coat. In a large skillet over medium heat, melt butter. Add chicken pieces and brown for 12 to 15 minutes per side. Remove chicken and reserve. Pour off and discard butter from skillet. Add remaining ingredients and stir to combine. Return chicken to skillet. Cover and cook over low heat for about 1/2 hour, turning chicken several times until cooked through. FRUIT AND NUT CHICKENServes 4 Inflation hits all of us, but in this recipe, you'll find one ingredient has come down in price over the years. In fact, it's come down spectacularly. In Roman times, raisins weren't just expensive, they were money. You could buy a young slave for 2 amphora (jars) of raisins. 2 tablespoons oil 1 chicken cut in serving pieces 1-1/2 cups orange juice 1 teaspoon salt or to taste 1/4 teaspoon cinnamon Ground pepper to taste 1/2 cup golden raisins 1/2 cup slivered almonds In a large skillet over medium heat, heat oil. Add chicken and brown for 12 to 15 minutes per side. Pour orange juice over chicken. Sprinkle salt, cinnamon, pepper, raisins and almonds on top. Cover and simmer for approximately 30 minutes or until cooked through. OVEN BARBECUED CHICKENServes 4 This isn't new or unique, but it's good. Of course, you can always use your favorite prepared barbecue sauce if you prefer. 1 chicken, cut in serving pieces 1 teaspoon salt or to taste 1/4 cup water 1/4 cup chili sauce 1/4 cup vinegar 2 tablespoons Worcestershire sauce 1/4 cup brown sugar 2 tablespoons oil Preheat oven to 350oF. Place chicken in single layer, skin side up, in shallow baking pan. In a mixing bowl combine remaining ingredients and pour over chicken. Bake, uncovered, for about 1 hour, or until cooked through. PHOTO: Drumsticks in bowl of rice - bread & glass of wine - 3 RECIPES WITH GROUND CHICKEN Ground Chicken is a perfect substitute for ground beef in dishes such as spaghetti, chili, meatloaf, lasagna or even plain burgers. And ground chicken has fewer calories and less fat than ground beef. It will vary according to the individual manufacturer's formulations, but ground chicken usually averages 60% less fat than the U.S. Department of Agriculture standard permits for regular ground beef. (Regular ground beef is about 30% fat.)

I was surprised to learn that there's actually a double standard for the beef industry and the poultry industry when it comes to describing fat content. Beef can be classified as "lean" at 22.5% fat, while chicken is only "lean" if it contains 10% or less fat.

I was also surprised to learn how complicated it is to make ground chicken. If I weren't connected with the industry, I would have thought that to get ground chicken, you just put it in a grinder the way you do to get hamburger, and that would be it. Ah, but it's not so! The fibers of chicken meat are shorter and more delicate than beef. To get the right texture took a full year of experimentation and fine tuning at Perdue. The skilled and knowledgeable food scientists working on the project had to discover which parts of the bird tasted best in hamburger, what size holes the meat should be forced through in the grinding machine, what temperature would be best, and so on. A difference of a mere 2 degrees in the meat's temperature meant the difference between a desirable texture and one that was merely passable.

I remember when the food scientists were first developing the ground chicken, that hundreds of people, including me, were involved in the taste testings. I also remember the first time Frank and I tried ground chicken outside of the laboratory. It happened at a barbecue at his son's house. Jim and Jan Perdue had chicken hamburgers and beef hamburgers grilling side by side, and Frank beamed like a kid with a new toy when he saw how the chicken burgers stayed plump and didn't shrink. Meanwhile the hamburgers, being 20% fat, were dwindling into hockey pucks. Basic Cooking Guide for Burgers: Saute: Shape one package fresh ground chicken into patties. Saute in a small amount of oil over high heat, 1 to 2 minutes on each side to brown. Reduce heat to medium and continue to cook 5 to 6 minutes on each side until thoroughly cooked and springs back to the touch. Broil: Shape one package fresh ground chicken into patties. Broil on a rack 4-inches from heat 5 to 6 minutes on each side until thoroughly cooked and springs back to the touch. Grill: Shape one package fresh ground chicken into patties. Place burgers on hottest area of lightly oiled grill 1 to 2 minutes on each side to brown. Move burgers toward the outside of the grill and continue to cook 5 to 6 minutes on each side until thoroughly cooked and springs back to the touch. CHICKEN STROMBOLI Serves 4 I've had this at a restaurant, made with bread dough, but I liked it better using this recipe with pie crust dough. The day I made it, I was late (as usual), and took a short cut: I used prepared pie crusts, the kind that come frozen and already shaped in aluminum pie pans. 2 tablespoons olive oil 1-1/2 cups thinly sliced onion 1 large green pepper, thinly sliced 1 package (about 1 pound) fresh ground chicken 1/4 cup tomato paste 1 clove garlic, minced 1 teaspoon dried oregano 1 teaspoon salt 1 prepared recipe pie crust mix 2 tablespoons butter or margarine, melted In a large skillet over medium-high heat, heat oil. Add onion and pepper and saute 3 to 5 minutes. Add chicken, tomato paste and seasonings and cook 8 to 10 minutes until chicken is cooked through. Preheat oven to 375oF. Roll out prepared pie crust into a round 1/8 inch thick. Cut circle in quarters to form 4 wedge shaped pieces. Place 1/4 of filling on the wide rounded end of each wedge; fold in sides and roll up. Place stromboli seam-side down on baking sheet, brush with butter and bake 30 minutes until pastry is lightly browned.

CHICKEN BURGERS BORDELAISEServes 4 These are good just as they are, but I've also found that they're wonderful made into little cocktail sized meat balls to pass during parties. By the way, at one of my parties, I tried to determine whether it was better to use the maximum amount of pepper and mustard in this recipe or the minimum. Some guests liked the meat balls highly seasoned, and others preferred them mild, so I guess one isn't better than the other; it's just what your family or guests like. 1 package (about 1 pound) fresh ground chicken 1 to 1-1/2 teaspoons coarsely ground black pepper 1 tablespoon vegetable oil (optional) 1-1/4 cups red wine 1/4 cup minced shallots or scallions 1 tablespoon sugar 2-3 teaspoons Dijon mustard 1/4 teaspoon dried thyme 1 to 2 tablespoons butter or margarine 1 tablespoon minced fresh parsley Form chicken into 4 burgers. Press pepper into both sides. In a large, non-stick skillet, over medium-high heat, heat oil. Add burgers and brown for 2 minutes on each side. Salt burgers lightly and reduce heat to medium-low. Continue cooking 5 to 6 minutes per side until thoroughly cooked through. While burgers are cooking, combine wine, shallots, sugar, mustard and thyme in a saucepan. Cook over high heat 5 to

6 minutes until liquid is reduced to 3/4 cup. Remove burgers from skillet and keep warm. Add wine mixture to skillet and stir over medium heat to combine with pan juices. Whisk in butter and parsley. Spoon sauce over burgers and serve.

RECIPES WITH THIGH & DRUMSTICKS If you haven't liked dark meat up until now, try these recipes with an open mind. Thigh meat, drumsticks, or the meat from any well-exercised muscle, has more flavor and is apt to be juicier. If Frank were going by taste alone and forgetting about calories, he would always choose thigh meat. I was present at a taste testing at Perdue when Teri Benson, a Food Technician, asked the dozen or so participants to rate the flavor of various parts of a chicken. The chicken was ground and fried in patties so none of us could identify which parts we were eating. We also couldn't be influenced by what our neighbors thought because each patty was coded and the breast meat or the thigh meat on my plate was in a different position from what they'd be on my neighbor's plate. The test was replicated with many different groups, but the results were fairly uniform: people prefer the flavor and juiciness of thigh meat. Try a few of these recipes; you may discover some new family favorites. WALDORF SALADServes 4 You could use other apples in this recipe, such as Red Delicious or Granny Smith, but the McIntosh with its characteristic crispness, juiciness, and mildly tart flavor works particularly well in this recipe. You can tell a McIntosh by its two-toned red and green skin. 1 quart chicken broth 4 roaster boneless thigh cutlets 1/4 cup fresh lemon juice 1 teaspoon Dijon mustard 1/4 cup vegetable oil 2 tablespoons minced, fresh parsley Salt and ground pepper to taste 1/2 cup celery, thinly sliced 1 to 2 McIntosh apples, unpeeled in 1/2-inch cubes (about 1 cup) 1/2 cup walnut halves 1 head Bibb or Boston lettuce In a 2 quart saucepan over medium heat, bring chicken broth to a boil. Add chicken and simmer over low heat for 30 minutes, uncovered. Drain thighs and cut into bite-size pieces. Reserve broth for other use. In a mixing bowl blend together lemon, mustard, oil, parsley, and salt and pepper. Toss warm chicken with sauce and allow to cool. Toss with remaining ingredients and serve on beds of Bibb or Boston lettuce.

DRUMSTICKS WITH HERB SAUCE

Serves 2

When serving this recipe, take a tip from Bev Cox, a woman who not only is responsible for many of my favorite Perdue recipes over the years, but who is also famous for being one of the best food stylists around. She likes to have the garnishes mirror the seasonings, so if she had, for example, this chicken recipe with basil in it, she'd be apt to garnish it with fresh basil. She also believes that garnishes should be edible. These chicken drumsticks with new potatoes and green beans would be a simple dinner, but sprinkle the new potatoes with chopped chives, stick a red pepper ring around the green beans and you have something that looks special as well as tastes special.

5 roaster drumsticks
salt and ground pepper to taste
1 clove garlic, minced
2 tablespoons olive oil

Sauce:
1/4 cup minced fresh basil, or 1 tablespoon dried
1/4 cup minced, fresh parsley
1/4 cup thinly sliced scallions
2 tablespoons white vinegar
1 tablespoon minced fresh tarragon, or 1 teaspoon dried
1 tablespoon capers
1/4 cup olive oil

Preheat oven to 375oF. Place drumsticks in a baking pan and season with salt and pepper. In a small bowl combine garlic and olive oil and baste drumsticks generously. Bake drumsticks for 60 to 75 minutes until tender and cooked through, turning and basting once. Meanwhile, in a bowl make sauce by whisking together remaining ingredients. Serve drumsticks, passing sauce separately.

DRUMSTICKS ZINGARA

Serves 2

The word "zingara" is from a French sauce with mushrooms, ham, and truffles. In this version, I've skipped the truffles.

5 roaster drumsticks
3/4 cup (3-ounces) minced fresh mushrooms
3/4 cup (1/4 pound) minced ham
1/2 cup minced shallots or scallions
3 tablespoons Madeira or brandy, divided
1 1/2 teaspoons minced, fresh tarragon, or 1/2 teaspoon dried
4 tablespoons butter or margarine, softened, divided
salt and ground pepper to taste

Preheat oven to 375oF. Pull back the skin of each drumstick and cut lengthwise slits in the meat in 4 places. Pull skin back into place In a mixing bowl, combine mushrooms, ham, shallots, 1 tablespoon Madeira, tarragon, 3 tablespoons butter and salt and pepper. Stuff mixture under the skin of each drumstick and secure with toothpicks. Melt remaining butter and baste drumsticks. Bake for 60 to 75 minutes or until tender and cooked through. Remove to a serving platter and remove toothpicks. To drippings in pan, add 2 tablespoons Madeira and bring to a boil, stirring. Pour sauce over drumsticks.

CHILI THIGHS RELLENOS If you're making this recipe and you're not sure how old the eggs you have in your refrigerator are, the chances are that they're still good. As long as they're clean, dry, have been kept cold and have no cracks, and weren't cooked, they'll last for months in your refrigerator and still be suitable for cooking in dishes like this. Eggs that are several months old won't have the quality of a perfectly fresh egg, and I wouldn't use them for frying, but they're still edible. Do be sure they've been kept cold and have no cracks and are clean. 4 roaster boneless thigh cutlets 1 can (4-ounces) whole, mild green chilies, seeded 1 egg, beaten salt and ground pepper to taste 1/2 cup seasoned bread crumbs 1 tablespoon butter or margarine 1 tablespoon olive oil 1 can (8-ounces) tomato sauce 1/2 cup shredded Monterey Jack Cheese Open thighs and lay flat. Divide chilies in four equal amounts and place in the center of each thigh. Roll up and secure with toothpicks. In a shallow bowl, combine egg and salt and pepper to taste. Dip thighs in egg and roll in bread crumbs. Refrigerate 15 minutes. In a large skillet, over medium heat, melt butter with oil. Add thighs and cook, turning, 10 to 12 minutes or until brown on all sides. Spoon tomato sauce over thighs. Reduce heat to medium-low reduce heat and cover. Cook for 20 minutes or until thighs are cooked through. Sprinkle with cheese; cover and cook 2 minutes longer. INDONESIAN STIR-FRY THIGHSServes 4 This recipe originally called for much more ginger, but I like a milder flavor, so I reduced it. You may want to increase the amount suggested here if you like highly seasoned food. To store fresh ginger, keep it in the refrigerator in a plastic bag along with a dampened paper towel to keep it from drying out. 4 roaster boneless thigh cutlets 2 tablespoons peanut or vegetable oil 1/3 cup soy sauce, divided 3 tablespoons molasses 3 tablespoons rice wine or white distilled vinegar 2 teaspoons minced, fresh ginger or to taste 1 clove garlic, minced 1/4 teaspoon salt or to taste 1/4 teaspoon red pepper flakes or ground pepper pinch ground cloves 1/8 teaspoon nutmeg 1 teaspoon cornstarch 1 cup carrots, cut in match stick strips 1 cup peeled cucumber, halved, seeded and cut into match- stick strips 1/2 cup thinly sliced scallions Cut thighs into 1/8-inch strips. In a wok or large skillet over medium-high heat, heat oil. Add chicken and stir-fry for 2 minutes Add 4 tablespoons soy sauce, molasses, vinegar, seasonings, garlic and ginger; bring to a boil. Cover, reduce heat to medium-low and steam chicken 5 minutes, stirring once, until tender. In a small bowl dissolve cornstarch in remaining soy sauce and reserve. Add carrots and steam, covered, 2 minutes. Stir in cucumber, scallions and cornstarch mixture and stir until liquid comes to a boil. Serve over hot fluffy rice. ISLAND THIGHSServes 4 One of the best money-saving tips I know for buying food is one you can use in this recipe. A Pennsylvania mushroom grower told me that when you see slightly browned mushrooms on sale$and they're often a fraction of the price of the cosmetically perfect mushrooms$buy them. The mushroom flavor will be more intense since the mushrooms are older; they'll have dried slightly so you won't be paying as much for water; and you won't see the discolorations anyway if you're using the mushrooms for cooking. I've tried his recommendation many times, and I think he's right. 4 roaster boneless thigh cutlets 3 tablespoons cornstarch 2 tablespoons vegetable oil 1 cup sliced fresh mushrooms (4 ounces) 1 cup thinly sliced scallions 1 cup chicken broth 1-1/2 cups fresh snow peas or 1 package (6 ounces) frozen snow peas, thawed 3/4 cup seedless, green grapes, halved 2 teaspoons slivered lemon peel 1 teaspoon minced, fresh ginger, or 1/4 teaspoon ground Cut thigh cutlets into 1/4" by 2" strips. Toss with cornstarch to coat well. In a wok or large skillet, over medium-high heat, heat oil. Add chicken and saute until browned on all sides, 3 to 4 minutes. Add mushrooms and scallions. Saute, stirring until mushrooms are golden, about 1 minute. Stir in remaining ingredients. Cook, stirring, until sauce is thickened and smooth. Reduce heat and simmer 1 to 2 minutes. Serve over rice. POJARSKI STYLE THIGHSServes 4 Pojarski style dishes use ground meat. They are typically made from beef, veal, salmon, or chicken. One of the most famous Pojarski dishes is salmon shaped to look like a pork chop. Doing the same thing with chicken tastes and looks delicious and costs a lot less. 1 package fresh ground chicken (about 1 pound) 1/2 cup sour cream, divided salt and ground pepper to taste 1/8 teaspoon nutmeg 1/2 cup flour 2 tablespoons butter or margarine 1 cup sliced fresh mushrooms (4 ounces) 2 tablespoons minced fresh dill or parsley Mix ground chicken with 1/4 cup sour cream, plus salt and pepper to taste. Cover and refrigerate 15 minutes. Form mixture into four "chop" shaped cutlets and coat each lightly with flour. In a large skillet over medium heat, melt butter. Add cutlets and saute for 7 to 8 minutes on each side until lightly browned and cooked through. Remove to a serving dish and keep warm. Add mushrooms to skillet and saute 2 to 3 minutes. Add remaining sour cream and mix well. Spoon sauce over cutlets. Sprinkle with fresh dill. STIR-FRIED THIGHS WITH BEANSPROUTSServes 4 Stir frying isn't more difficult than regular frying, but one big difference is that the pan is kept hotter than would be usual for American-style frying. To tell if it's hot enough, place your frying pan$or wok if you have one$over high heat. The pan or wok is hot enough if a drop of water dropped onto it sizzles and then evaporates. Add the oil, and let the oil heat until it's almost at the smoking point. When adding the ingredients, stir them constantly until done. 4 roaster boneless thigh cutlets 1 tablespoon cornstarch 1 egg white, slightly beaten salt to taste 2 to 3 tablespoons peanut oil, as needed 1 or 2 cloves garlic, minced 1 red, sweet, bell pepper, cut into thin strips 1/2 cup thinly sliced scallions 1/4 pound (2 cups) snow peas, sliced diagonally 1/2 pound (4 cups) beansprouts, washed and drained 1/4 cup soy sauce few drops Tabasco, to taste Cut thighs into 1/4" strips. In a shallow bowl, combine cornstarch, egg white and salt. Add chicken, turning to coat well. Cover and refrigerate one hour. In a wok or large skillet over high heat, heat 1 tablespoon oil. Add thighs and garlic and stir-fry for 3 minutes. Remove chicken and set aside. Add additional oil to wok, if necessary. Add pepper strips and stir-fry one minute. Remove and set aside. Add scallions and snow peas and stir-fry one minute. Add beansprouts and cook, tossing, 2 minutes. Return chicken and pepper to wok and toss. Add soy sauce and Tabasco. Heat thoroughly. Serve over hot cooked rice. SWEET AND SOUR THIGHSServes 4 Cornstarch yields a more transparent sauce, and has roughly twice the thickening power of flour. The transparency makes it appropriate for oriental recipes like this one. 4 roaster boneless thigh cutlets 2 tablespoons peanut oil 1 1/2 cups sliced green pepper 2/3 cup sliced celery 1/2 cup sliced scallions, stems included 1 can (8-1/2-ounces) sliced water chestnuts, drained 6 ounces fresh or frozen (thawed) snow peas 1 can (8-3/4-ounces) pineapple chunks in syrup 1/2 cup chicken broth 1 tablespoon cornstarch 2 tablespoons sugar 1 1/2 teaspoons minced fresh ginger or 1/2 teaspoon ground 2 tablespoons vinegar 2 tablespoons soy sauce Cut thighs into bite size pieces. In a wok or large skillet, over medium-high heat, heat oil. Add thigh pieces and stir-fry 5 minutes. Add green pepper, celery, scallions and water chestnuts. Stir-fry 2 minutes. Add snow peas, pineapple and syrup and chicken broth. Reduce heat to medium and cook for 2 minutes, stirring often. In a small bowl, blend together cornstarch, sugar, ginger, vinegar and soy sauce. Add to wok and cook until sauce is slightly thickened, about 2 minutes. Serve over hot cooked rice. SZECHUAN STIR-FRY THIGHSServes 4 The woman in charge of supervising the entire Perdue recipe program, says that this is her personal favorite. 4 roaster boneless thigh cutlets 4 tablespoons peanut or vegetable oil 1 cup carrots, cut into matchstick strips 1/2 cup cashews 1 teaspoon hot chili pepper, finely chopped, or to taste 1 clove garlic, minced 2 teaspoons minced fresh ginger 1/4 cup soy sauce 1/4 cup dry sherry 1 tablespoon cornstarch Cut boneless thighs into strips (about 1/4" x 2"). In a wok or large skillet over high heat, heat 2 tablespoons oil. Add chicken and stir-fry for 2 to 3 minutes. Remove chicken and reserve. Add remaining 2 tablespoons oil to wok and add carrots, cashews, chili pepper, garlic and ginger. Stir-fry 3 minutes until carrots just begin to soften. Return chicken to wok. In a small bowl blend together soy sauce, sherry and cornstarch. Add to wok and cook, stirring constantly, until sauce boils and thickens. Serve over hot cooked rice. THIGH CHILIServes 4 This is a healthy, low-cholesterol chili. 4 roaster boneless thigh cutlets 2 tablespoons vegetable oil 1/2 cup chopped onion 1 large garlic clove, minced 1 green pepper, seeded and chopped 1 can (16-ounces) tomatoes, chopped, with liquid 1 can (16-ounces) kidney beans, drained 1 tablespoon chili powder salt and ground pepper to taste Tabasco, to taste Cut chicken into bite size pieces. In a Dutch oven over medium-high heat, heat oil. Add chicken, onion, garlic and green pepper and cook, stirring until chicken loses its pink color. Add remaining ingredients and stir. Simmer, covered, over medium-low heat for 30 minutes or until chicken is tender. Adjust seasonings according to taste. THIGH FLAUTASServes 4 You can tell if your avocado for the guacamole in this recipe is ripe by whether it yields to gentle pressure when you hold it between your palms. If there's some "give" to it, it's ripe. If it feels hard, like a baseball, it's not ripe. Wait a few days, and it will have a richer, creamer texture and flavor. You can speed the ripening by keeping the avocado in a paper bag, at room temperature, along with a banana or pear or apple. These fruits give off a ripening factor and the paper bag concentrates the ripening factor. 4 roaster boneless thigh cutlets 1 quart chicken broth 1/2 pound Monterey Jack or Cheddar cheese, coarsely grated (about 2 cups) 1/4 cup red or green chili salsa salt to taste 8 flour tortillas Vegetable oil, for frying 1/3 cup sour cream, optional Guacamole: 1 large ripe avocado 1 tablespoon fresh lemon or lime juice 1/2 cup chopped tomato 1/4 cup chopped onion 1 tablespoon red or green chili salsa In a large saucepan over medium-high heat bring chicken broth to a boil. Add boneless thighs, reduce heat to medium-low and simmer, uncovered, 30 minutes. Remove thighs, reserving broth for other use. Shred meat and place in a mixing bowl. Toss with 1-1/2 cups cheese, salsa, and salt to taste. Divide mixture among tortillas and roll up, securing with a toothpick, if necessary. In a large, heavy skillet over medium-high heat, heat 1/2-inch oil. Fry flautas in hot oil, turning to brown lightly on all sides. Transfer to serving dish and keep warm. To make guacamole, scoop out avocado flesh, chop and toss with lemon juice. Combine lightly with remaining ingredients. Serve flautas topped with guacamole, remaining cheese and sour cream, if desired. Chapter Two. Chicken for the Microwave

When I was organizing this chapter, I was tempted to include all of these microwave recipes in the "Cooking for Everyday" chapter. After all, the microwave is certainly becoming part of our everyday life.

The reason I didn't is$well, there are two reasons. First, if I put all the microwave recipes in one chapter, you won't have to waste time hunting for them. Second, there are a number of tips on using the microwave successfully, and I thought you might like to have them all in one place, also.

The microwave is a wonderful convenience, but in my case, I used to use it for reheating foods or for boiling water and not much else. Are you the same? Ah, but there's so much more to it than that! Having spent time with the Perdue food technologists and home economists, and especially after studying the techniques and recipes from Rita Marie Schneider, the home economist who developed the majority of the Perdue microwave recipes,

I'm a convert now. I've come to appreciate the versatility of the microwave as well as the speed.

There's a reason I happen to have spent time with the Perdue experts. Once when Frank was microwaving nuggets for himself at HIGH, he found that by the time all of them were heated, one of them was badly overcooked and therefore, dried out and$what a dirty word this is in the Perdue household!$tough. Frank didn't know that the microwave was the problem and instead assumed it was his product that was at fault.

How can I even tell you about the crisis that one tough "tender" caused! Frank didn't seem as upset when a whole processing plant burned down the year before. Because of that one tough tender, he called the plant manager, the quality control people, the packaging people, the man who wrote the cooking directions, the food technologists, the woman who runs the tasting lab, and probably half a dozen other people as well. It didn't matter that it was the weekend$the situation had to be addressed immediately! He kept repeating disconsolately, "I have no right to sell a product like this."

Eventually, one of the Perdue food technicians came out to our house and checked the microwave and suggested that we'd get more even cooking if we used MEDIUM HIGH. She said that at this setting, the microwaves reach an equilibrium so heating is much more even. And when there are no hot spots and no cold spots, the chicken gets uniformly warm with no dried out tough parts.

While she was there, she had a number of other tips for me as well, and as I talked with other Perdue people, I collected still more. By now, knowing a few little tricks about the microwave, I know how to make much better use of it. Because of the time it saves in cooking, and the time it saves in clean-up (no baked on bits of food to scrub), I use the microwave about as often as my oven.

Tips for Using Your Microwave

_The best microwave tip I know is, learn about the "cold spots" in your microwave so you don't end up with unevenly cooked chicken. To learn your microwave's "cold spots," line the bottom of your microwave oven with wax paper and then spread an eighth-inch layer of pancake batter over it. Turn the oven on HIGH, and then check it at 30 second intervals. At some point, (in my case after a minute and a half), you'll see that in some places the batter is dried out and hard, while in others, it's still soupy, as if the heat hadn't touched it. Once I made this check, I gained an immense respect for the fact that microwaves don't necessarily cook evenly, and I've made sure to compensate ever since by stirring or turning foods as directed in microwave recipes.

_Do not use utensils with metal trim (including the gold trim on fine china), handle clamps, or fastening screws. Metal trim can cause arcing (sparking). Aluminum foil, in small amounts on the other hand, won't cause arcing in most microwaves as long as it doesn't touch the sides of the oven.

_The coverings used in microwave cooking have definite purposes: use plastic wrap to steam and tenderize; use wax paper to hold in heat without steaming; use paper towels to absorb moisture, yet hold in heat.

_To obtain a crisp, crunchy crumb-coated chicken, first cook covered with wax paper, then switch to a paper towel covering and, finally, complete cooking with chicken uncovered.

_If the bony parts of your chicken are overcooking before the meatier parts are done, shield the bony parts by placing strips of thin aluminum foil over them.

_If you're microwaving chicken livers, prick each one to allow steam to escape. Before I knew this tip, I've had them explode in the oven.

_Microwave recipes usually call for smaller amounts of seasonings than conventionally cooked dishes. Microwaving tends to intensify flavors, so you won't need as much seasoning.

_Don't ignore the standing time called for in some of these recipes. In microwave cookery, standing time allows further cooking to occur after you have removed the food from the microwave oven. Covering the food holds heat in and speeds this final, important step. When I've cheated on this step, I've found the chicken hard to carve and undercooked.

_When possible, arrange food in a circular or donut shape; without corners, food cooks more evenly from all sides. For example, if you're cooking drumsticks, arrange them like a wagon wheel with the meatier portions at the outer edge, and the drum stick end in the center.

_Thin foods cook faster than thick foods because microwaves lose power after they penetrate food.

_Ingredients also affect cooking time. Foods higher in sugar or fat heat faster and to higher temperatures than do those with lower sugar or fat content.

_When the recipe says "70% power," or MEDIUM HIGH, don't be tempted to get things done faster by going for 100% power. At 70% power, the microwaves cook the product more slowly but also more evenly, so there's less worry about cold spots.

ROASTED CHICKEN WITH ALMOND SAUCEServes 4 Of course you can serve the pre-cooked chicken just as it comes from the store, without doing anything else to it at all. I've done this many times with our Perdue Done It! roasted chicken when I've been in a hurry. But this recipe only takes a few extra minutes and you'll have a show piece at the end. As you're making it, be glad for a moment that you're not making this recipe in the year 1911. A typical recipe in a the December issue of The Wisconsin Farmer assumes that you've already plucked the bird and removed its head and feet. It directs you "to singe the bird over a burning newspaper on a hot stove." The stove would probably have been a wood-burning one, and in all probability, it would have been up to you to get the wood for the stove. When I think of then and I think of now, I'm glad that "We've come a long way, baby". 1 roasted chicken 1 tablespoon cornstarch 1 cup chicken broth 2 tablespoons Amaretto or other almond liqueur 1-1/2 teaspoons fresh lemon juice 1/4 cup sliced toasted almonds Heat pre-cooked roasted chicken in its own microwave tray following package directions. In 2-cup glass container, combine cornstarch, broth, liqueur and lemon juice. Cover with plastic wrap and microwave at HIGH (100% power) 3 or 4 minutes until bubbly and thick; stir twice during cooking. Add almonds. Slice chicken onto a platter and top with sauce.

FIVE-MINUTE ROASTED DRUMSTICKS 1 package roasted chicken drumsticks (4-6 per package). Following package directions, warm roasted drumsticks in a conventional oven or, using package tray, heat in a microwave oven. Brush with your favorite bottled barbecue sauce.

CHICKEN POCKET SANDWICHESServes 4 You could use regular chicken breasts for this, but the roaster breast has a richer, more chickeny flavor. ("Chickeny" is a word, by the way. Frank uses it all the time, and he ought to know.) 1 roaster boneless breast 1/4 cup olive oil 2 tablespoons fresh lemon juice 2 tablespoons finely chopped onion 1 clove garlic, minced 1/2 teaspoon salt or to taste 1/2 teaspoon dried oregano 1/8 teaspoon Cayenne pepper 4 pita breads Lettuce leaves 1 container (8-

ounces) plain yogurt 3 tablespoons finely chopped green onion Cut chicken into 1-inch chunks. In 3-quart microwave-safe utensil, combine olive oil, lemon juice, onion, garlic, salt, oregano, and Cayenne pepper; add chicken chunks and stir. Cover with wax paper; microwave at HIGH (100% power) 10 minutes or until chicken has turned white. Stir mixture 3 or 4 times during cooking. Let stand, covered, 5 minutes. Cut each pita bread into 2 pockets, line with lettuce and spoon in chicken. In small bowl, combine yogurt and green onion; serve over chicken.

CHICKEN A LA MONTMORENCY Serves 6 Any recipe with the word "Montmorency" is apt to have cherries in it. The sauce for this one is particularly good and Frank liked it enough to spread the leftovers on toast the next day at breakfast. If you don't want to microwave the roaster breast, just cook it in your oven, following the package directions. When I'm in a hurry, I use this microwave recipe, but breasts are the hardest part of the chicken to keep tender in a microwave because they're fairly dry to begin with, and if you overcook them, they'll get tough. 1 roaster breast 1 can (16-ounces) pitted dark sweet cherries 1/4 cup dry red wine Water 5 teaspoons cornstarch 2 tablespoons red currant jelly (optional) 1 tablespoon butter or margarine Salt and ground pepper to taste Place breast, skin side down, on microwave-safe roasting utensil. Cover with wax paper; microwave at HIGH (100% power) 5 minutes. Reduce power to MEDIUM HIGH (70% power) and cook 12 minutes per pound. Halfway through cooking time, turn breast, skin side up; brush with drippings in utensil. Re-cover with wax paper; complete cooking. Let stand, covered, 15 minutes. Test for doneness after standing; juices should run clear with no hint of pink when breast is cut near bone. Drain cherries, reserving syrup in a 4-cup glass container. Place cherries and red wine in small bowl. Add enough water to cherry syrup to measure 1 cup. Stir in cornstarch, mixing until well blended. Microwave at HIGH 3 minutes, stirring twice. Stir cherries with wine into thickened syrup. Continue cooking at HIGH 1 to 2 minutes or until mixture thickens and boils for 1 minute. Add jelly, if desir ed, and butter; stir until smooth. To serve, slice chicken and place on warm platter. Spoon some of cherry sauce over chicken slices; pass remaining sauce.

CHICKEN A LA NANCYServes 4 Unlike me, Frank does not enjoy puttering around in the kitchen. He loves the results, but cooking is not his favorite way to spend his free time. (He'd be more apt to watch a game on TV or visit with friends.) When he does cook, I can almost guarantee that it will be something quick and carefree. But there is one exception, and it's this recipe. I've never dared ask just who Nancy is, but Frank once won a cooking contest using her recipe, so he's been fond of it ever since. He says to point out that the cooked lemon with rind does remain as a part of the food. It adds an unusual taste and texture. If you don't like a strong lemony flavor, you might start by using half the lemon that the recipe calls for. That's what I do when I make this recipe. 4 skinless, boneless chicken breast halves or 1 thin sliced boneless roaster breast 1 tablespoon vegetable oil 1 clove garlic, minced 1/2 lemon with peel, very thinly sliced 1/2 pound fresh mushrooms, sliced 1/4 cup dry white wine 1 tablespoon flour 1/2 teaspoon salt or to taste 1/4 teaspoon ground pepper 1/4 teaspoon dried oregano 1 can (14-ounces) water-packed whole artichoke hearts, drained and quartered Place chicken breasts between sheets of plastic wrap. Pound to 1/4 inch thickness and cut into 2 inch squares. If using thin sliced boneless Roaster breast, skip the pounding and simply cut into 2 inch squares. Frying Pan Method: In a large skillet over medium heat, hat oil. Add garlic and saute until soft. Add lemon and mushrooms and saute 1 to 2 minutes. Add all other ingredients except artichokes. Fry, stirring frequently, approximately 15 minutes or until chicken is cooked through. Add artichokes and heat. aMicrowave Method: In 3-quart microwave-safe round dish, combine oil, mushrooms, lemon slices and garlic; cover with plastic wrap. Microwave at HIGH (100% power) 3 minutes, stirring once. In a 1-cup glass measuring cup, combine wine and flour; stir into mushroom mixture. Arrange chicken pieces on top of mushroom mixture and cover with wax paper. Microwave at MEDIUM-HIGH (70% power) 6 minutes per pound, stirring mixture 3 times. Sprinkle with salt, pepper and oregano. Stir in artichoke quarters; re- cover and microwave at HIGH 2 minutes. Let stand, covered, 5 minutes.

CHICKEN THIGHS PARMESANServes 3-4 The Dijon mustard called for in this recipe is quite sharp before it's cooked. After heating in the microwave, you'll find that it loses much of its sharpness and leaves behind a subtle spicy flavor. Yellow mustard won't produce the same effect. 6 chicken thighs 1/2 cup seasoned bread crumbs 1/4 cup grated Parmesan cheese 1/4 cup melted butter or margarine 1 tablespoon Dijon mustard 1 1/2 teaspoons Worcestershire sauce Remove skin from thighs. On wax paper, combine bread crumbs and Parmesan cheese. In shallow dish, combine butter, mustard and Worcestershire sauce. Brush thighs with butter mixture and then roll in crumbs to lightly coat both sides. Reserve remaining butter mixture and crumbs. Arrange thighs in circular pattern on microwave-safe roasting utensil; cover with wax paper. Microwave at MEDIUM-HIGH (70% power) 10 minutes per pound. Halfway through cooking time, turn thighs over; spoon on remaining butter mixture and sprinkle with remaining crumb mixture. Cover with a double thickness of paper towels. Complete cooking; remove paper towels during last 2 minutes cooking time. Let stand, uncovered, 2 minutes before serving.

CHICKEN WITH MANGO SAUCEServes 6 Mangos, which are rich in vitamins A and C, make a delicious, colorful and unusual sauce for a roaster breast. When mangos aren't available, try fresh or canned peaches. 1 roaster breast 1 tablespoon butter or margarine 1 tablespoon cornstarch 2 tablespoons brown sugar 1/2 cup fresh orange juice 2 ripe mangos, peeled and cut into chunks 2 tablespoons cherry- or orange-flavored liqueur Salt and pepper to taste Place skin side down on microwave-safe roasting utensil. Cover with wax paper; microwave at HIGH (100% power) 5 minutes. Reduce power to MEDIUM-HIGH (70% power) and cook 12 minutes per pound. Halfway through cooking time, turn breast skin side up; brush with drippings in utensil. Re- cover with wax paper and complete cooking. Let stand, covered, 15 minutes. Test for doneness after standing; juices should run clear with no hint of pink when breast is cut near the bone. In a 4-cup glass container, place butter. Microwave at HIGH 30 seconds or until melted. Stir in cornstarch until blended; stir in brown sugar and orange juice. In blender or food processor fitted with steel blade, puree mango chunks. Stir pureed mangos into orange juice mixture. Microwave at HIGH 4 minutes, stirring twice. Add liqueur; microwave 1 minute longer. To serve, slice chicken and place on warm platter. Spoon some of mango sauce over slices, then pass remaining sauce.

CURRY-GLAZED BREASTServes 4 Curry powder is a blend of many spices, so you don't need to combine spices yourself. Indian Curry Powder is mild and Madras Curry Powder is quite hot. 1 whole roaster breast 2 tablespoons butter or margarine 1/4 cup honey 2 tablespoons Dijon mustard 2 teaspoons curry powder 1/4 teaspoon salt or to taste Place breast bone side down on a microwave-safe roasting utensil. Place butter in a 2-cup glass container; microwave at HIGH (100% power) 45 seconds. Stir in honey, mustard, curry powder and salt; brush mixture all over breast. Cover with wax paper; microwave at MEDIUM-HIGH (70% power) 12 minutes per pound. Baste breast and rotate utensil 3 or 4 times during cooking. Let stand, covered with wax paper, 15 minutes. Test for doneness after standing; juices should run clear with no hint of pink when breast is cut near bone.

HAM AND CHICKEN ROLL-UPSServes 4 If you can't easily find the prosciutto called for in this recipe, substitute any thinly sliced ham, such as the pre- sliced ham you find in the deli section of your supermarket. Or try thin slices of smoked turkey ham. If you slice the cooked Roll-Ups crosswise, they make wonderful hors d'oeuvres or appetizers. 4 skinless, boneless chicken breast halves or 1 thin sliced boneless roaster breast 1 tablespoon olive oil 1 teaspoon dried rosemary, crumbled Salt and ground pepper to taste 4 thin slices prosciutto Place chicken breast halves between 2 sheets of plastic wrap and pound to 1/2-inch thickness. Skip the previous step if you are using thin sliced boneless roaster breasts. Brush breasts with olive oil to help seal in moisture; sprinkle with rosemary, salt and pepper. Roll up each breast half, starting from narrow end. Wrap a slice of prosciutto around each roll. In 8-inch square microwave-safe baking dish, place chicken rolls seam side down. Cover with wax paper. Microwave at HIGH (100% power) 8 minutes, rotating dish 2 or 3 times during cooking. Let stand 5 minutes. Check for doneness after standing; juices should be clear with no hint of pink when chicken is cut near center.

HEAVENLY CHICKENServes 4 If you're using fresh asparagus spears for this, here's how to tell the tender part from the part that's too tough and fibrous to be good eating. Take the bud end of an asparagus spear in one hand and the butt end in the other and then bend the spear until it breaks. The part on the bud side is tender enough to use. The spears will always break at just that point. But don't throw away the tough end. If you peel the tough end with a potato peeler, you'll get down to the tender, edible part underneath and can use that portion also. Cook the leftover parts until tender and use them in soups or omelettes. 4 chicken breast halves 12 fresh or frozen asparagus spears 1/4 cup water 1/4 cup butter or margarine 4 tablespoons flour 1/8 teaspoon ground ginger 1 1/2 cups chicken broth 1/2 cup dry white wine Salt and freshly ground pepper to taste 1/4 cup chopped pecans 1/4 cup crushed crackers On microwave-safe roasting pan, arrange breasts, bone side up, in a circular pattern. Cover loosely with plastic wrap; microwave at MEDIUM-HIGH (70% power) 8 minutes per pound. Halfway through cooking time turn breasts over; re- cover with plastic wrap and complete cooking. Let stand, covered, 10 minutes. Rinse asparagus and remove tough end. On microwave-safe rack, arrange asparagus with stem ends toward outside. Place rack in microwave-safe utensil. Add water; cover with plastic wrap. Microwave at HIGH (100% power) 5 to 7 minutes or until tender-crisp. Let stand, covered, 3 to 5 minutes. In 4-cup glass container, place butter; microwave at HIGH 1 minute. Blend flour and ginger into melted butter. Gradually add chicken broth, wine, salt and pepper, stirring constantly. Microwave at HIGH 5 minutes or until thick and smooth, stirring 3 times. In 12 x 8-inch microwave-safe dish, arrange cooked asparagus, with stem ends toward outside; pour half of wine sauce over asparagus. Arrange chicken breasts on top with meatier portions toward outside; spoon remaining sauce over breasts. Sprinkle pecans and cracker crumbs on top; cover with a double thickness of paper towels. Microwave at MEDIUM-HIGH 5 minutes or until heated through.

MICROWAVE MARMALADE DRUMSTICKSServes 4 This recipe calls for a microwave-safe utensil. Do you know how to tell for sure if your utensil is suitable?

1. Place the utensil and a cup of water side by side in the microwave oven.

2. Turn the oven to the HIGH setting for 1 minute. If the dish is warm, then it is absorbing microwave energy. Do not use it in the microwave oven. 5 roaster drumsticks 2 tablespoons butter or margarine 3/4 cup finely chopped onion 1/2 cup orange marmalade (You can also use current jelly) 1/2 teaspoon curry powder In 9-inch microwave-safe utensil, combine butter and onion. Cover; microwave at HIGH (100% power) 5 minutes. Blend in marmalade and curry powder; turn drumsticks in mixture. Place drumsticks with meatier portions toward outer edge of utensil; cover with wax paper. Microwave at MEDIUM-HIGH (70% power) 12 minutes per

pound. Halfway through cooking time, turn chicken over, re-cover with wax paper and microwave remaining time. Let stand, covered, 15 minutes.

SAUCY MICROWAVE CHICKEN WINGS Serves 4 To make an attractive presentation, try tucking the tip of each wing under to form a triangle. 1/2 cup honey 1/4 cup soy sauce 2 tablespoons ketchup 1 small clove garlic, minced 16 chicken wings In 12 x 8-inch microwave-safe utensil, combine all ingredients except wings; turn wings in mixture. Cover with wax paper. Microwave at MEDIUM-HIGH (70% power) 8 minutes per pound, turning wings over 3 to 4 times during cooking. Let stand, covered, 10 minutes.

TEX-MEX DRUMSTICKS Serves 4 Removing skin from chicken is an easy way to reduce calories, and because moisture doesn't evaporate readily in microwave cooking, the chicken will remain juicy and flavorful. 6 chicken drumsticks 1/4 cup finely chopped pecans 1/4 cup fine, dry bread crumbs 1 tablespoon minced fresh parsley 1 teaspoon chili powder 1/4 cup taco-flavored or other pourable salad dressing Remove skin from drumsticks. On wax paper, combine pecans, bread crumbs, parsley and chili powder. Brush drumsticks with taco dressing, then roll in crumb mixture to coat all sides. Reserve crumbs and dressing. On microwave-safe roasting pan, arrange drumsticks in circular pattern, with meatier portions toward outside. Cover with wax paper; microwave at MEDIUM-HIGH (70% power) 10 minutes per pound. Halfway through cooking time, turn drumsticks over, spoon on remaining dressing and sprinkle with reserved crumb mixture. Cover with a double thickness of paper towels. Complete cooking, removing paper towels during last 2 minutes. Let stand, uncovered, 5 minutes before serving.

MICROWAVE CHICKEN BREASTS PAPRIKASH Serves 4 One way of avoiding having your eyes tear when the slicing the onion in this recipe is to do the cutting under running tap water. The vapors that hurt your eyes won't have a chance to get into the air, but instead will just wash down the drain. 2 tablespoons vegetable oil 2 green peppers, thinly sliced 1 large onion, thinly sliced 1 can (8-ounces) tomato sauce 1 tablespoon sweet paprika 1/2 teaspoon dried marjoram 1/2 teaspoon salt or to taste Ground pepper to taste 4 chicken breast halves 1 container (8-ounces) commercial sour cream 1 tablespoon flour In a 12 x 8-inch microwave-safe utensil, combine oil, peppers and onion. Cover with plastic wrap; microwave at HIGH (100% power) 5 minutes. Stir in tomato sauce, paprika, marjoram, salt, and pepper. On top of tomato mixture, place breasts bone side up with meatier portions toward outside. Cover with wax paper; microwave at HIGH 5 minutes; reduce power to MEDIUM-HIGH (70% power) and cook 10 minutes per pound. Halfway through cooking time, turn breasts over and stir mixture. Re-cover with wax paper and microwave remaining time. Let stand 5 minutes. Stir sour cream and flour into tomato mixture. Cover; microwave at HIGH 1 minute. Stir and let stand 2 minutes. Pour over chicken breasts.

CORNISH HENS WITH LEMON TARRAGON SAUCEServes 4 You can get more juice from a lemon if you roll it around on a flat surface first while pressing your palm against it fairly hard. This ruptures the little juice sacks. You'll also get more juice if the lemon is at room temperature rather than just out of the refrigerator. 2 fresh Cornish game hens 1/4 cup flour 1 1/2 teaspoons fresh tarragon, divided, or 1/2 teaspoon dried 1 cup chicken broth Juice of one lemon (about 1/4 cup) Salt and ground pepper to taste 1/2 pound fresh asparagus, or substitute green beans 2 teaspoons water With sharp knife or poultry shears, cut hens in half, lengthwise. Remove and discard backbone and skin. Coat hen pieces lightly with flour and sprinkle with half of tarragon. Place hens bone side up, with legs to inside, on a microwave-safe roasting utensil. In a 4-cup glass container, combine chicken broth, lemon juice, remaining tarragon and pepper. Microwave at HIGH (100% power) 3 to 4 minutes, or until boiling. Baste hens with half of hot broth. Cover with wax paper; microwave at MEDIUM-HIGH (70% power) 10 minutes per pound combined weight of hens. Halfway through cooking time, turn hens bone side down and baste with remaining broth mixture. Re- cover and complete cooking. Let stand, covered, 10 minutes. Slice asparagus diagonally into 1-inch pieces and place in a 2-quart microwave-safe utensil with water. Cover; microwave at HIGH 3 TO 4 minutes. Let stand 2 minutes; drain and set aside. When ready to serve, add asparagus to lemon sauce and pour over hens.

MICROWAVE HENS JUBILEEServes 2 This is a close cousin of CHICKEN A LA MONTMORENCY, but it's spicier and less sweet. 2 fresh Cornish game hens 1 can (16-ounces) dark sweet cherries in syrup 1/4 cup dry sherry 2 tablespoons cornstarch 1/2 cup chili sauce 1 clove garlic, minced Salt and freshly ground pepper to taste With poultry shears or sharp knife, split hens lengthwise, removing backbone, if desired. In 12 x 8 microwave-safe utensil, arrange hens, bone side up with meatier portions to outside. In 2-quart microwave-safe utensil, drain liquid from cherries; blend in sherry and cornstarch. Add cherries, chili sauce, garlic, salt and pepper. Microwave at HIGH (100% power) 3 to 4 minutes, stirring once, until mixture begins to boil and thicken. Pour sauce over hens. Cover loosely with wax paper. Microwave at MEDIUM-HIGH (70% power) 8 minutes per pound, turning the hens over halfway through cooking time. Re-cover with wax paper and microwave remaining time. Let stand, covered, 10 minutes.

PINEAPPLE BAKED CORNISH HENSServes 4 Green peppers and most other fresh vegetables are ideal for microwaving. They retain their clear color and stay crunchy and fresh tasting. For extra color, substitute 1/2 sweet red pepper and 1/2 green pepper for the single whole green pepper. 2 fresh Cornish game hens 1 green pepper, cored, finely chopped 1 medium onion, finely chopped 2 teaspoons vegetable oil 1 can (8-ounces) crushed pineapple in natural juices 2 tablespoons soy sauce 2 teaspoons dry mustard 1/2 teaspoon ground ginger With poultry shears or sharp knife, split hens lengthwise and remove and discard skin. Place hens bone side up on a microwave-safe 12 x 8-inch utensil, arranging with legs to inside. In a 2-quart microwave-safe utensil, place green pepper, onion and oil. Microwave at HIGH (100% power) 2 to 3 minutes or until pepper is tender. Add pineapple, soy sauce, mustard and ginger; microwave at HIGH 1 to 2 minutes. Baste hen halves with half of pineapple mixture. Cover with wax paper. Microwave at MEDIUM-HIGH (70% power) 10 minutes per pound combined weight of hens. Halfway through cooking time, turn hens bone side down and baste with remaining pineapple mixture. Re-cover and complete cooking. Let stand, covered, 10 minutes. Serve with pineapple sauce.

ROSEMARY HENS WITH LIGHT WINE GRAVYServes 4 Game hens are sold both fresh and frozen. If you've selected a frozen one, follow your microwave manufacturer's directions for defrosting and turn and rearrange the birds frequently for even defrosting. I've tried game hens both fresh and frozen, and I found that there's enough of a difference in flavor and tenderness to make me strongly prefer fresh. 2 Cornish game hens 6 sprigs fresh parsley 1 small onion, halved 1 clove garlic, halved 3 small carrots, peeled, cut in 1/2-inch slices (1 cup) 2 medium tomatoes, peeled and cut in wedges, or 6 cherry tomatoes, halved 1 medium zucchini, cut in 3/4-inch slices (1 cup) 1/4 pound mushrooms, quartered (about 1 cup) 1/2 cup chicken broth 1/4 cup dry white wine 1 and 1/2 teaspoon minced, fresh rosemary or 1/2 teaspoon dried Salt and freshly ground pepper to taste 2 tablespoons cold water 2 teaspoons cornstarch Into each hen cavity, place 3 sprigs parsley, 1/2 onion and 1/2 garlic clove. Place carrots, tomatoes, zucchini and mushrooms in a microwave-safe baking dish. Combine chicken broth, wine and 1/4 teaspoon rosemary; pour over vegetables. Cover with plastic wrap and microwave at HIGH (100% power) 5 minutes.

Arrange hens, breast side down, on top. Sprinkle with remaining rosemary and pepper. Cover with wax paper. Microwave at MEDIUM-HIGH (70% power) 11 minutes per pound combined weight of hens. Halfway through cooking time, stir vegetables; turn hens breast side up and rotate dish. Re-cover with wax paper. Remove hens to serving platter, reserving juices for gravy. Using slotted spoon, arrange vegetables around hens and cover with foil; allow to stand 10 minutes. Cut hens in half to serve. To prepare gravy, in a 4 cup glass container, combine water and cornstarch. Slowly add reserved cooking juices (about 3/4 cup) from hens; stir to blend. Microwave at HIGH 2 minutes or until thickened, stirring twice. Serve with Cornish hens.

HONEY MUSTARD ROASTERServes 8 Covering is a key technique in successful microwave cooking. In a conventional oven a sweet honey-mustard basting sauce could overbrown. Instead, in the microwave it dries as the roaster skin cooks and it forms an attractive golden glaze on the bird. 1 whole roaster (about 6 pounds) 4 tablespoons butter or margarine 1/2 cup honey 1/4 cup Dijon mustard 1/4 teaspoon curry powder 1 teaspoon salt or to taste 1/8 teaspoon ground pepper Remove giblets from roaster. With rounded wooden picks, fasten skin across cavity and neck openings. Place roaster, breast side down, on microwave-safe roasting pan. Melt butter in a 1-cup glass measuring cup by microwaving at HIGH (100% power) 1 minute. Stir in honey and remaining ingredients; brush roaster with mixture and cover with wax paper. Microwave at HIGH 5 minutes. Reduce power to MEDIUM-HIGH (70% power) and cook 12 minutes per pound, brushing frequently with honey mixture. Halfway through cooking time, turn roaster breast side up; complete cooking. Let stand, covered, 20 minutes. Test for doneness after standing; juices should run clear with no hint of pink when thigh is pierced. Pour drippings from utensil into remaining sauce mixture in measuring cup; microwave at HIGH 2 minutes or until heated through. Serve sauce with roaster.

MEXICAN MICROWAVE CHICKEN CASSEROLE Leftover Mexican Chicken Casserole makes a fast and delicious taco filling. Shred chicken, reheat in sauce and serve with shredded lettuce and cheese and a dollop of sour cream. 2 tablespoons butter or margarine 1 large onion, chopped (1 cup) 1 large green pepper, chopped (1 cup) 1 clove garlic, minced 1 can (14.5 ounces) tomato sauce 2 tablespoons flour 1 teaspoon salt or to taste 1/2 teaspoon ground cumin 1/2 teaspoon dried oregano 1/4 teaspoon ground pepper 1 chicken cut in serving pieces 1 can (17-ounces) corn, drained In 3 to 5-quart microwave-safe utensil, combine butter, onion, pepper and garlic. Cover with plastic wrap; microwave at HIGH (100% power) 3 to 5 minutes or until onion and pepper are tender. Stir in tomato sauce, flour, salt, cumin, oregano and pepper. Place chicken pieces, bone side up with meatier portions toward outside of utensil, on top of mixture. Cover with wax paper; microwave at HIGH 5 minutes. Reduce power to MEDIUM-HIGH (70% power) and cook 10 minutes per pound. Halfway through cooking time, turn chicken pieces over; re- cover with wax paper and microwave remaining time. Let stand, covered, 10 minutes. Remove chicken pieces to serving dish; cover. Add corn to sauce in utensil; cover with plastic wrap. Microwave at HIGH 2 minutes. To serve, pour sauce over chicken.

PLUM-SPICED CHICKENServes 4 The plum sauce is a low-fat way to make the chicken develop an attractive color as it cooks in the microwave. 1 chicken, cut in half lengthwise 1 cup plum jelly or preserves 1/2 cup chicken broth 1/4 cup chopped onion 3 tablespoons red wine vinegar 1 1/2 teaspoons soy sauce 1/2 teaspoon ground ginger 1/2 teaspoon Chinese five-spice powder (optional) Place chicken halves, skin side down, on microwave-safe roasting utensil, set aside. In a 4-cup glass container, combine jelly and remaining ingredients. Microwave at HIGH (100% power) 4 minutes, stirring 3 times. Brush chicken halves with sauce; cover with wax paper. Microwave at MEDIUM-HIGH (70% power) 10 to 12 minutes per pound, brushing chicken frequently with sauce. Halfway through cooking time, turn chicken halves over; brush with sauce. Re-cover with wax paper; complete cooking. Let stand, covered 15 minutes.

STUFFED CHICKEN CHARLESTON STYLE Serves 4 The microwave oven makes it possible to make this succulent roast chicken and all the trimmings in less than an hour. To complete the meal with "baked" potatoes, you can microwave them during the chicken's standing time. 1 whole chicken 4 strips uncooked bacon, diced 1/4 cup chopped onion 1/4 cup chopped celery 1 1/2 cups packaged cornbread stuffing 1/4 cup coarsely chopped pecans 5 tablespoons butter or margarine, melted, divided 1/2 cup plus 2 tablespoons dry sherry, divided 2 tablespoons water 2 tablespoons minced fresh parsley 1 teaspoon salt or to taste Ground pepper to taste Remove giblets. In 1 1/2-quart microwave-safe utensil place diced bacon; cover with paper towel. Microwave at HIGH (100% power) 3 minutes or until crisp, stirring twice. With slotted spoon, remove bacon to paper towel to drain; set aside. Reserve drippings. In same 1 1/2-quart microwave-safe utensil, combine onion and celery; cover with plastic wrap. Microwave at HIGH 2 minutes. In a mixing bowl, combine onions and celery with stuffing, pecans, and cooked bacon. In cup, blend 2 tablespoons butter, 3 tablespoons sherry and water; toss with stuffing. Spoon stuffing loosely into cavity and neck openings of chicken. With rounded wooden picks, fasten skin across cavity and neck openings. Combine 1 tablespoon butter with 1 teaspoon sherry; brush on chicken. Place chicken, breast side down, on microwave- safe roasting utensil; cover with wax paper. Microwave at MEDIUM-HIGH (70% power) 10 minutes per pound, brushing chicken frequently with butter-sherry mixture and drippings. Halfway through cooking time, turn chicken breast side up; re-cover with wax paper. Complete cooking. Let stand, covered, 15 minutes. Test for doneness after standing; juices should run clear with no hint of pink when thigh is pierced Pour pan drippings into a 2-cup glass container. Add 1/2 cup sherry to roasting utensil to loosen pan juices; pour into container with drippings.

Microwave at HIGH 3 minutes; stir in remaining 2 tablespoons butter and parsley. Serve chicken, sliced, with stuffing and gravy.

CHEESY MICROWAVE THIGHS Serves 4 Chicken thighs and drumsticks are fairly uniform in size, making them an ideal choice for quick cooking in the microwave. 6 chicken thighs 4 tablespoons butter or margarine, divided 1 cup finely chopped onion 2 tablespoons flour 1/2 teaspoon salt or to taste 1 cup milk 1/2 cup grated Swiss cheese 1/4 cup grated Parmesan cheese 2 tablespoons white wine Pinch freshly grated or ground nutmeg Minced, fresh parsley (optional) Remove and discard skin from thighs. In a 12 x 8-inch microwave-safe utensil, combine 2 tablespoons butter and onion. Microwave at HIGH (100% power) 5 minutes. Arrange thighs in a circular pattern on top of onions. Cover with wax paper; microwave at MEDIUM-HIGH (70% power) 10 minutes per pound. Halfway through cooking time, turn thighs over; re-cover with wax paper and microwave remaining time. Let stand, covered, 10 minutes. Place remaining butter in 4-cup glass container; microwave at HIGH 30 to 50 seconds. Blend in flour and salt; gradually stir in milk, mixing well. Microwave at HIGH 3 to 5 minutes, stirring frequently, until mixture boils and thickens. Add cheeses, wine and nutmeg; stir until cheese is melted. Pour sauce over chicken thighs; cover with wax paper. Microwave at MEDIUM-HIGH 2 to 3 minutes or until heated through. Garnish with parsley if desired.

CHICKEN MARENGO Serves 3-4 Frank admires Napoleon because he was such an effective leader and motivator of men. But Frank has another reason to like the famous French general. Napoleon liked chicken so much that during his campaigns, he ate it almost every night. In 1800 when Napoleon was fighting in Italy, the supply wagons were late and his chef had to scour the countryside for whatever food he could find. The result was a chicken dish made with olive oil, mushrooms, tomato, garlic and other ingredients available from the nearby farms. Napoleon liked the dish so much that he named it "Chicken Marengo," in honor of the battlefield where he had just been fighting, and from then on ordered it served to him after every battle. 6 chicken thighs 2 teaspoons olive oil 2 cups coarsely chopped fresh plum tomatoes 1/2 cup chopped green pepper 1/4 cup finely chopped onion 2 cloves garlic, minced 2 tablespoons minced, fresh parsley 1/2 teaspoon dried oregano 1/4 teaspoon ground pepper 1/2 teaspoon salt or to taste Remove and discard skin from thighs. In 3-quart microwave- safe utensil, combine remaining ingredients; cover with plastic wrap. Microwave at HIGH (100% power) 5 minutes, stirring twice. Arrange thighs in circular pattern on top of tomato mixture; spoon mixture over thighs. Cover with wax paper; microwave at MEDIUM-HIGH (70% power) 10 minutes per pound. Halfway through cooking time, turn thighs over; re-cover and complete cooking. Let stand, covered, 10 minutes before serving.

CHINESE CHICKENServes 4 The shape of foods affects cooking results. Thin areas cook faster than thicker ones, so meatier portions should always be placed toward the outer edge of the utensil where microwave energy is greater. 4 chicken drumsticks 4 chicken thighs 1/4 cup melted butter 2 tablespoons soy sauce 1/4 teaspoon ground pepper 1/8 teaspoon minced, fresh ginger 1 can (3-ounces) chow mein noodles 1/4 cup sliced almonds Salt to taste Remove and discard skin from drumsticks and thighs. In small bowl, mix butter, soy sauce, pepper and ginger. In blender or food processor fitted with steel blade, finely chop chow mein noodles, almonds and salt; transfer to wax paper. Brush chicken with soy mixture, then roll in noodle mixture to coat all sides. Arrange on microwave-safe roasting pan, with meatier portions toward outside; cover with wax paper. Reserve remaining soy and noodle mixture. Microwave at MEDIUM-HIGH (70% power) 10 minutes per pound. Halfway through cooking time turn legs and thighs over; spoon on remaining soy mixture and sprinkle with remaining noodle mixture. Cover with a double thickness of paper towels. Complete cooking, remove paper towels during last 2 minutes. Let stand, uncovered, 5 minutes before serving.

DRUMSTICKS LITTLE ITALY STYLEServes 4 Do you know how to tell when rice is done? The aim of cooking rice is to have all the little starch granules inside each grain swell with water but not burst. You can tell that rice is undercooked if you pinch a grain and feel a hard or gritty core. You can tell that it's overcooked if you look at a grain closely and find that the edges are split and ragged. It's perfectly cooked if the grain is the same smooth shape as the uncooked grain, only puffed, swollen and soft. 1 cup chopped, canned tomatoes 3/4 cup long grain rice 1 cup chicken broth 1/2 cup dry white wine 1 medium onion, chopped 1 large clove garlic, crushed 1/2 teaspoon dried thyme 5 roaster drumsticks Salt and ground pepper to taste 2 tablespoons or more minced, fresh parsley In a 3 quart microwave-safe utensil combine tomatoes and rice. Stir in broth and wine; add onion, garlic, thyme, and mix well. Cover with plastic wrap; microwave at high (100% power) 5 minutes. Arrange drumsticks over top of mixture, with meatiest portions to the outer edge of utensil. Re-cover with plastic wrap; microwave at HIGH (100% power) 5 minutes then at MEDIUM-HIGH (70% power) 12 minutes per pound. Halfway through cooking time stir and turn drumsticks over. Re-cover and complete the cooking. Let stand, covered 10 minutes before serving. Test for doneness after standing; juices should run clear with no hint of pink when drumstick is pierced. Season with salt and pepper. Add parsley to rice mixture for garnish.

OLIVE MICROWAVED CHICKENMakes 6 Drumsticks When you saw the title of this recipe, did you hesitate because you were concerned that the calories in olives could wreck your diet? Not to worry! Olives are actually a fairly low calorie food, with the average one having only 4-5 calories. The largest jumbo olive has only 12 calories. 6 chicken drumsticks 1 cup slivered onion strips 1/2 cup slivered green pepper strips 1/2 cup thawed lemonade concentrate 1/2 cup ketchup 1/4 cup sliced pimento-stuffed olives 1/4 cup sliced pitted ripe olives 2 teaspoons Worcestershire sauce 1 clove garlic, minced Remove and discard skin from drumsticks. In a 12 x 8-inch microwave-safe utensil, combine remaining ingredients; cover with plastic wrap. Microwave HIGH (100% power) 5 minutes, stirring once. Turn drumsticks in sauce to coat. Arrange drumsticks in circular pattern in sauce with meatier portions toward outside of utensil. Cover with wax paper; microwave at MEDIUM-HIGH (70% power) 10 minutes per pound. Halfway through cooking time, turn drumsticks and spoon sauce on top. Re-cover with wax paper; complete cooking. Let stand, covered, 10 minutes before serving.

PENNSYLVANIA DUTCH-COUNTRY DRUMSTICKSServes 2 When you're buying the apples for this recipe, you can tell which ones are Red Delicious by looking at the base of the apples. A Red Delicious always has five knobs or points at the base. 5 roaster drumsticks Salt and ground pepper to taste 6 tablespoons butter or margarine, divided 1/2 cup apple juice (1/4 cup for microwave) 1 tablespoon soy sauce (1-1/2 teaspoons for microwave) 1/4 cup brown sugar, firmly-packed (1/8 cup for microwave) 2 Red Delicious apples, peeled, cored and cut into 8 wedges each 2 tablespoons sugar Conventional Method: Season drumsticks with salt and pepper. In a large skillet over medium heat, melt 3 tablespoons butter. Add drumsticks and brown for 4 to 5 minutes per side. In a measuring cup combine apple juice, soy sauce and brown sugar and pour over drumsticks. Cover and simmer 20 minutes. Turn and simmer 25 minutes longer. Ten minutes before end of cooking time, in another skillet, over medium-high heat, melt remaining butter. Add apple wedges and brown on one side. Sprinkle with sugar and turn. Brown other side. Transfer chicken to serving dish and top with apple wedges. Spoon sauce over top. aMicrowave Oven: Place 2 tablespoons of butter in a 9-inch microwave-safe utensil. Microwave at HIGH (100% power) 40 seconds. Combine 1/4 cup apple juice, 1 1/2 teaspoons soy sauce and 1/8 cup firmly packed brown sugar with melted butter. Place drumsticks in apple juice mixture and turn to coat well. Arrange drumsticks with meatiest portions toward outer edge of utensil. Cover with wax paper. Microwave at MEDIUM-HIGH (70% power) 12 minutes per pound. Half way through cooking time turn drumsticks and spoon sauce over each. Re-cover and complete cooking. Let stand, covered, 5 to 10 minutes. Place 2 tablespoons butter in a 2-quart microwave-safe utensil. Microwave at HIGH 40 seconds. Sprinkle butter with 2 tablespoons firmly packed brown sugar; stir. Place apple wedges in brown sugar mixture; toss gently to coat. Microwave at HIGH 3 minutes, stir. Microwave an additional 3 minutes or until apples are tender. Transfer chicken to serving dish and top with apple wedges. Spoon sauce over top.

ROASTER THIGHS IN WINEServes 4 For the longest shelf life and the best flavor, don't wash the mushrooms called for in this recipe until just before using them. And don't soak them, just lightly mist them or wipe them with a damp paper towel. With soaking, they easily become waterlogged and lose some of their flavor. 4 roaster boneless thigh cutlets 4 strips uncooked bacon, diced 1 cup Burgundy or other dry, red wine 2 tablespoons cognac or brandy 16 small whole onions, peeled 8 ounces sliced, fresh mushrooms, 2 cups 3 tablespoons flour 2 teaspoons minced fresh parsley 1 bay leaf 1 1/2 teaspoons minced, fresh thyme or 1/2 teaspoon dried Cut thigh cutlets in half. In 3-quart microwave-safe utensil, place bacon; microwave at HIGH (100% power) until crisp, 3 to 4 minutes. Combine wine and Cognac and add to utensil with remaining ingredients; stir well. Arrange thighs, with thicker portions toward outer edge, on top of vegetables. Cover with wax paper; microwave at HIGH 5 minutes. Reduce power to MEDIUM-HIGH (70% power) and cook 12 minutes per pound. Halfway through cooking time, stir vegetable mixture and turn cutlets over.

SPICY AFRICAN DRUMSTICKS Serves 4 If you eliminate the crushed pepper in this recipe, it could be a dish children would love. Be sure the peanuts you use in the recipe are fresh. Once a package has been opened, keep it in the refrigerator since peanuts rapidly go rancid. As an emergency first aid measure for peanuts that aren't as fresh as you wish they were, try this tip I got from a peanut farmer in Georgia. Put the peanuts in a sieve and pour boiling water over them. The hot water will wash away some of the oils that are responsible for the off-flavor. 6 chicken drumsticks 2 tablespoons vegetable oil 1 cup chopped onion 1 garlic clove, minced 1 can (16-ounces) tomato puree 1/2 teaspoon salt or to taste 1/8 teaspoon crushed red pepper 1/4 cup peanut butter 1/4 cup chopped peanuts Remove and discard skin from drumsticks. In a 12 x 8-inch microwave-safe utensil, combine oil, onion and garlic. Cover with plastic wrap; microwave at HIGH (100% power) 5 minutes or until onions are tender. Stir in tomato puree, salt and red pepper. Arrange drumsticks in utensil with meatier portion toward outside; spoon tomato sauce over top. Cover with wax paper; microwave at MEDIUM-HIGH (70% power) 10 minutes per pound. Halfway through cooking time, turn drumsticks over; re-cover with wax paper and microwave remaining time. Remove drumsticks to serving platter; cover with foil and let stand 10 minutes. Stir peanut butter and peanuts into tomato sauce. Cover with plastic wrap; microwave at HIGH 2 minutes. To serve, spoon sauce over drumsticks.

CORNUCOPIA STUFFED ROASTER Serves 8 A roaster stuffed with vegetables and rice is a tasty meal in one dish. The stuffing doesn't increase the cooking time, which is about one hour less in a microwave than required for conventional roasting. 1 whole roaster (about 6 pounds) 1/4 cup hot water 1/4 cup butter or margarine 1 cup frozen peas and carrots 1 1/2 cups cooked rice 2 tablespoons minced fresh parsley 1/2 teaspoon dried thyme 1 teaspoon salt or to taste Browning spray (optional) Remove giblets.

In a 1-cup glass measuring cup, place water and butter; microwave at HIGH (100% power) 1 minute. In 1-quart microwave-safe utensil, place peas and carrots; cover. Microwave at HIGH 4 minutes, stirring once; drain. In a small bowl, combine rice, melted butter mixture, peas and carrots, parsley, thyme and salt. Place in cavity of roaster; with rounded wooden picks, fasten skin across cavity opening and at neck. Place roaster, breast side down, on microwave-safe roasting pan. Spray with browning spray or brush roaster with melted butter if desired; cover with wax paper. Microwave at HIGH 5 minutes. Reduce power to MEDIUM-HIGH (70% power). Cook 12 minutes per pound, brushing with drippings several times during cooking. Halfway through cooking time, turn roaster over, using paper towels to protect hands. Pour off drippings and reserve, if desired. Baste roaster with drippings or use browning spray; cover with wax paper and complete cooking. Let stand, covered with aluminum foil, 20 minutes. Test for doneness after standing; juice should run clear with no hint of pink when thigh is pierced. To serve, spoon stuffing into serving bowl and slice roaster. CHICKEN WING PAELLAServes 4-6 Paella is a Spanish dish with a mixture of rice, vegetables, meat and sometimes shellfish. I lived in Spain for a couple of years and came to the conclusion that there must be almost as many versions of Paella as there are Spanish cooks$which means that you have a lot of latitude to vary the ingredients according to what you have handy in your refrigerator. I like this better the next day, when the different flavors have had a chance to "marry." 10 chicken wings 1 pound sweet Italian sausage links 1 teaspoon browning sauce 1 large onion, chopped 1 sweet red pepper, cut into thin strips 1 medium-sized zucchini, chopped 1 can (16-ounces) tomatoes, undrained 1/2 cup hot water 1 teaspoon salt or to taste 1 teaspoon dried oregano 1/2 teaspoon paprika 1/2 teaspoon ground turmeric 1/2 teaspoon Tabasco 2 cups hot cooked rice 1 cup frozen peas, thawed Cut wing-tip section from wings. Set tips aside to cook later in soup or stew, if desired. Brush sausages with browning sauce; cut into 1-inch pieces. In 3-quart microwave-safe dish, place sausage pieces; cover with wax paper. Microwave at HIGH (100% power) 6 to 7 minutes, or until sausage loses its pink color, stirring twice. With slotted spoon remove sausage. To drippings in dish, add onion, red pepper and zucchini; cover with plastic wrap. Microwave at HIGH 5 minutes, stirring twice. Add tomatoes, browned sausages, water, salt, oregano, paprika, turmeric and Tabasco; stir to blend. Arrange chicken wings in circular pattern on top of tomato mixture. Cover with plastic wrap; microwave at HIGH 5 minutes. Reduce power to MEDIUM-HIGH (70% power); cook 10 minutes per pound. Halfway through cooking time, turn wings over; re-cover and complete cooking. Stir in hot cooked rice and peas; microwave at HIGH 3 minutes. To warm for serving, cover with plastic wrap to speed cooking and microwave at HIGH until heated through. Let stand 5 minutes before serving.

CHAPTER THREE-CHICKEN FOR DIETERS

Are you concerned about the cholesterol in your diet?
Are you watching calories and trying to cut down on fat?
Has your doctor suggested that you consume less salt?

Then read on. The wonderful thing about chicken is that the low cholesterol and the low calorie recipes are the same. And the flavors that add spark to a low calories recipe are the same ones that can help you get along with little or no salt.

Chicken is the dieter's ray of sunshine. Except for turkey breast, no other popular meat is as low in calories as skinless chicken breast. A 3-ounce portion of skinless broiled chicken breast has only 115 calories. An equivalent size portion of cooked lean trimmed beef would average 189 calories, and cooked lean, trimmed pork is 198 calories.

Chicken is also lowest in saturated fat compared with non-poultry meats.

Grams of Saturated Fat
Cooked 3-ounce portion skinless chicken breast: 0.4
Average cooked 3-ounce portion of chicken: 1.1
Average cooked 3-ounce portion of lean, trimmed beef: 3.4
Average cooked 3-ounce portion of lean, trimmed pork: 3.8

To avoid both fat and calories when cooking with chicken:

_Choose breast meat. This is the leanest part of the bird and has less than half the fat of, for example, thigh meat. Because of its low fat content, it's the only meat I ever serve Frank, and it's the only meat he ever asks for in restaurants.

_Remove the skin. Forty percent of the fat in poultry is attached to the skin and therefore can be easily removed. This is in contrast with other meats, where the fat is dispersed throughout the meat and not so easily removed. One point, though. If you're broiling or baking or grilling chicken, leave the skin on until you're finished cooking; otherwise the meat will lose too much moisture and become tough. I've watched tests done at the Perdue Tenderness Laboratory in which they measured the tenderness of breast meat roasted with the skin and without the skin. The meat cooked with the skin retained its moisture and was startlingly more tender than the meat cooked without the skin.

_Roast, broil, poach, or grill chicken instead of frying it.

_Substitute low fat dairy products in recipes. Use yoghurt or light sour cream instead of sour cream, and non- fat milk instead of regular milk. To be honest, the taste isn't as rich, but if you're watching calories and cholesterol, these substitutions make a substantial difference. For example, plain low fat yoghurt is 122 calories per cup and light sour cream about 360 calories, while the same amount of regular sour cream is 440 to 454 calories. Non-fat milk is 80 to 90 calories per 8-ounce glass, while whole milk is 150 to 160 calories.

_Replace oil or fat in marinades with fresh lemon or lime juice, or with wine or vinegar.

_Broil with wine instead of butter.

_Take advantage of non-caloric pan sprays.

_If you're really counting every single calorie, you may want to choose Cornish hens rather than the older broilers and roasters. Cornish hens and broilers are young birds and they bear the same relationship to the older roasters that veal does to beef: the younger the animal, the lower the fat content. For comparison, the white meat of a Cornish is 35 calories per ounce of cooked meat; the white meat of a broiler is 45 calories per cooked ounce. For low salt diets:

_Avoid prepared sauces such as barbecue sauce or ketchup: usually they are high in salt.

_Season chicken with foods that are naturally high in potassium, such as tomatoes, citrus, raisins or bananas. When you eat foods high in potassium, you don't miss the sodium so much. Tomato paste, by the way, is very high in potassium, and does not have as much added salt as most prepared or canned foods.

_Season foods with garlic, onion, wine and a variety of herbs and spices. Again, you'll miss the sodium less.

_Trick your palette by cooking with your own flavored vinegars. Use a cup of whichever fresh herb you can find, such as tarragon or mint or dill, for two cups of plain white vinegar and then add a garlic clove or twist of lemon peel. Store in a screw top jar for several days and if you want it really strong, leave it for a week. You might taste it along the way to see if it's too strong. Finally, strain it and pour into a sterilized bottle and seal.

_Season chicken with concentrated homemade chicken broth. Make chicken stock (use the recipe on page ___, but omit the salt), boil it down until it's concentrated, and then freeze it in ice cube trays. Use individual cubes to intensify the flavor of casseroles or stir fry dishes.

After a couple of weeks of following a low salt diet, you'll find that your taste changes and that you'll actually be satisfied with far less salt. You'll even find that the olives and potato chips and peanuts that once tasted just right, now seem too salty. We've found that with salt, the less you eat, the less you feel you need$but be patient because this doesn't happen overnight.

For that matter, a preference for low fat cooking may not happen overnight either. In fact, to level with you, I think that in most cases it won't happen overnight. If you're not used to the low fat substitutions for rich sauces and gravies, some of the recipes in this chapter may seem downright Spartan to you the first time you try them. But once you're used to them, you may find as Frank and I have, that with time it's not only possible to get used to lighter cooking, it's actually possible to prefer it.

BARBECUE DRUMSTICKSServes 8 Microwave Recipe To save additional fat and calories, remove the skin from the drumsticks. I wouldn't recommend this for a conventional oven recipe because the meat would dry out. But microwaving retains moisture, and the sauce adds flavor. 8 roaster drumsticks 1 cup water 1/2 cup finely chopped onion 1/3 cup tomato paste 1 tablespoon vinegar 2 cloves garlic, minced 1-1/2 teaspoons chili powder 1 teaspoon dry mustard 1/4 teaspoon ground pepper Remove skin from drumsticks and discard. In 4-cup glass container, combine water, onion, tomato paste, vinegar, garlic, chili powder, mustard and pepper until well blended. Cover with plastic wrap; microwave at HIGH (100% power) 5 minutes. Stir and microwave, uncovered, 5 minutes longer. Pour half the mixture over bottom of a 12 x 8-inch microwave-safe utensil. Place drumsticks in sauce with meatier portions toward outer edge of utensil. Pour remaining sauce over drumsticks; cover with wax paper. Microwave at

MEDIUM-HIGH (70% power) 12 minutes per pound. Halfway through cooking time, turn drumsticks over and move drumsticks to sides of utensil. Re-cover with wax paper; complete cooking. Let stand, covered, 15 minutes before serving. Nutritional Figures Per Serving Calories 94. Protein 16 grams. Carbohydrate 3 grams. Fat 2 grams. Cholesterol 51 mg. Sodium 142 mg. BURGUNDY CHICKENServes 4 Microwave Recipe The Perdue home economists say that microwave recipes are often more nutritious than their conventional versions because microwaving requires much less liquid, ensuring that vitamins and minerals are not washed away. 1 chicken, cut in serving pieces 1/2 cup Burgundy or other dry red wine 1/2 cup low-sodium chicken broth 1 teaspoon dried thyme leaves 1/4 teaspoon ground pepper 1 bay leaf 1/2 pound pearl onions, peeled 1/4 pound small mushrooms, sliced 8 small new potatoes, cut into quarters 2 carrots (about 1 cup), thinly sliced 2 tablespoons water 1-1/2 tablespoon cornstarch Remove and discard skin and visible fat from the larger chicken pieces. In a 3-quart microwave-safe utensil, combine wine, chicken broth, thyme, pepper, and bay leaf. Add onions, mushrooms, potatoes, and carrots. Cover and microwave at HIGH (100% power) 5 minutes. Arrange chicken on top of vegetables, bone-side up, with meatier portions toward outer edge of utensil. Cover with wax paper; microwave at HIGH 15 minutes. Turn chicken pieces over and rearrange, spooning vegetable mixture over each piece. Re- cover; microwave 5-6 minutes per pound or until chicken and vegetables are fork tender. Remove chicken pieces and vegetables; cover to keep warm. In microwave-safe cup, combine water and cornstarch. Add small amount of hot pan juices to cup and stir to blend; gradually stir cornstarch mixture into remaining juices. Microwave on HIGH 2 minutes; stir and microwave 2 minutes longer or until boiling. Serve sauce over chicken and vegetables. Nutritional Figures Per Serving Calories 438. Protein 42 grams. Carbohydrate 29 grams. Fat 17 grams. Cholesterol 122 mg. Sodium 137 mg. CHICKEN AU POIVREServes 4 Pepper's piquant flavor helps disguise the lack of salt. 1 roaster boneless breast or 1 package thin sliced roaster breast 2 tablespoons flour 2 teaspoons cracked black pepper 1 teaspoon dry mustard 2 tablespoons vegetable oil 1 clove garlic, minced 1/2 cup dry red wine 1 tablespoon minced, fresh parsley Remove and discard visible fat from boneless breast; slice thin. (You can skip this step if you have the thin sliced roaster breast.) Place chicken slices between sheets of plastic wrap and pound to 1/8 inch thickness. On wax paper, combine flour, pepper and mustard. Lightly coat chicken with flour mixture, pressing to make pepper adhere. In large skillet over medium-high heat, heat oil. Add garlic; saute 30 seconds. Place chicken in skillet so that pieces do not touch. Cook about 3 minutes or until lightly browned, turning once. Remove to serving platter; keep warm. Pour off fat; stir in wine. Cook over high heat, stirring constantly 2 to 3 minutes or until thickened and liquid is reduced by one-half. Stir in parsley. Spoon sauce over chicken.

Nutritional Figures Per Serving
Calories 255. Protein 36 grams. Carbohydrate 5 grams.
Fat 9 grams. Cholesterol 90 mg. Sodium 81 mg.

CHICKEN PROVENCALServes 4 Microwave Recipe Do you know why you brown chicken first in traditional stews and casseroles? It's to seal in the juices. You don't need to in microwave cooking, so you save the fat calories from the butter or margarine or oil you'd use for browning, and the chicken still ends up moist and tender. 4 chicken breast halves 3 cups coarsely chopped fresh Italian plum tomatoes

or a 28-ounce can, drained 1-1/2 cups sliced mushrooms (12-ounces) 1/3 cup chopped onion 1 clove garlic, minced 1/2 teaspoon dried basil 1/4 teaspoon salt or to taste 1/4 teaspoon ground pepper 2 tablespoons dry white wine 1 tablespoon cornstarch 2 tablespoons minced fresh parsley Remove and discard skin from chicken breasts. In a 3-quart microwave-safe utensil, combine tomatoes, mushrooms, onion, garlic, basil, salt and pepper. Cover with wax paper. Microwave at HIGH (100% power) 5 minutes. Meanwhile, in cup combine wine and cornstarch, stir into tomato mixture. Place chicken breasts, bone-side up and meatier portions toward outside of utensil, on top of tomato mixture. Cover with wax paper; microwave at HIGH 5 minutes. Reduce power to MEDIUM-HIGH (70% power) and cook 10 minutes per pound. Halfway through cooking time, turn chicken breasts over and stir tomato mixture. After cooking, let stand, covered, 10 minutes. Remove chicken to serving platter; stir parsley into tomato mixture and spoon some over breasts; serve remaining sauce on side.

Nutritional Figures Per Serving Calories 347. Protein 63 grams. Carbohydrate 13 grams. Fat 4 grams. Cholesterol 152 mg. Sodium 283 mg.

CHICKEN RATATOUILLEMakes 6 drumsticks. When "ratatouille" appears in a recipe's name, you can be sure it will have eggplant in it and probably tomatoes and peppers as well. These vegetables will be noticeably more delicious if you use them very fresh rather than after storage in the refrigerator. The flavor of these vegetables all deteriorate at refrigerator temperatures. They're warm weather crops and nature didn't mean for them to be in the chilling temperatures of a refrigerator. 6 chicken drumsticks 2 tablespoons vegetable oil 1 cup coarsely chopped onion 1 clove garlic, minced 1/2 pound eggplant, peeled and cubed 2 medium zucchini (about 1/2 pound) cubed 2 medium tomatoes, coarsely chopped 1 green pepper, cut in thin 1-inch strips 1 tablespoon minced, fresh basil or 1 teaspoon dried 3/4 teaspoon minced, fresh oregano or 1/4 teaspoon dried 1/4 teaspoon ground pepper Remove and discard skin and visible fat from drumsticks. In large skillet, over medium-heat, heat oil. Add drumsticks; cook about 15 minutes, turning until browned on all sides. Remove drumsticks; drain on paper towels. Add onion and garlic; cook 1 minute, stirring frequently. Add eggplant, zucchini, tomatoes, green pepper, basil, oregano and pepper. Cook

5 minutes, stirring occasionally. Place drumsticks in vegetable mixture; cook about 30 minutes longer or until drumsticks are tender, occasionally spooning vegetables over chicken.

Nutritional Figures Per Drumstick Calories 126. Protein 12 grams. Carbohydrate 8 grams. Fat 6 grams. Cholesterol 33 mg. Sodium 41 mg.

CHICKEN IN MUSTARD SAUCE Serves 4 If controlling sodium is important to you, use an ordinary table wine for the white wine called for in this recipe. Cooking wines often contain salt and should be avoided by anyone who is watching sodium intake. Likewise, sweet wines and fortified ones such as sherry, Madeira and Marsala should be used sparingly because they are higher in calories than dry wines. No wines contain alcohol after cooking. 1 roaster boneless breast or 1 package thin sliced roaster breast 3 tablespoons vegetable oil, divided 1/2 pound mushrooms, sliced (2 cups) 2 tablespoons minced, fresh parsley 1 tablespoon minced shallot or scallion 1/8 teaspoon ground pepper 1/2 cup low-sodium chicken broth 1/4 cup dry white wine 1 tablespoon Dijon mustard Remove and discard visible fat from breast; slice thin. (If using thin sliced product, skip this step.) In a large skillet over medium-high heat, heat 2 tablespoons oil. Add breast slices a few at a time, placing so that pieces do not touch. Saute 4 minutes, turning once, until chicken is lightly browned on both sides. Remove from skillet; keep warm. Heat remaining oil. Add mushrooms, parsley, shallot and pepper. Stirring frequently, cook 2 minutes. Stir in broth and wine; bring to a boil and cook until liquid is reduced by half (about 1/3 cup). Reduce heat to low; stir in mustard until well blended. Spoon over chicken.

Nutritional Figures per Serving Calories 286. Protein 37 grams. Carbohydrate 4 grams. Fat 13 grams. Cholesterol 90 mg. Sodium 201 mg.

CHICKEN VERONIQUE Serves 4 Any recipe with the name Veronique will have grapes in it. When buying grapes at the supermarket, you can tell how fresh they are by how green and pliable the stem is. Another way of telling is to give the bunch a quick shake. If it's fresh, none of the individual grapes should fall from the bunch. I should warn you, though, that shaking the bunch will not do anything for your popularity with the store's produce manager. 4 skinless, boneless chicken breast halves or 1 thin sliced boneless roaster breast 1/2 lemon Ground pepper 1 tablespoon unsalted margarine 1-1/2 teaspoons cornstarch 1/2 cup low-sodium chicken broth 1/4 cup dry white wine 1 cup seedless green grapes, halved Remove and discard any visible fat. Butterfly breast halves to make scaloppine. Skip the previous step if you are using thin sliced boneless roaster breasts. Rub with lemon and sprinkle lightly with pepper. In large skillet over medium heat, melt margarine. Add scaloppine, in batches if necessary, so that they do not touch. Saute 4 minutes, turning once, until chicken is lightly browned on both sides and just cooked through. Remove from skillet; keep warm. In small bowl, stir together cornstarch, broth and wine until smooth; add to skillet. Over medium heat, bring to boil; boil 1 minute, stirring constantly. Stir in grapes until heated through. To serve, spoon grapes and sauce over chicken.

Nutritional Figures Per Serving Calories 233. Protein 36 grams. Carbohydrate 9 grams. Fat 5 grams. Cholesterol 90 mg. Sodium 87 mg.

CHICKEN BREASTS WITH VEGETABLESServes 4 Whenever possible, choose crisp, fresh vegetables over their canned or frozen counterparts. Fresh vegetables have better color, flavor and texture. When using frozen or canned products, be sure to look for those with no salt added. This kind of nutritious, high vitamin, low calorie meal that features breast meat is a mainstay for Frank and me, and it has been for him for a long time. His grown daughter, Bev Nida, tells me that one of her childhood memories of Frank was that if he was late for dinner, ("and he always was"), everyone knew to save a chicken breast for him.

4 chicken breasts halves 2 tablespoons unsalted margarine 2 large carrots, cut into matchstick strips (1-1/2 cups) 2 ribs celery, cut into matchstick strips (1-1/2 cups) 1 green pepper, cut into matchstick strips (1 cup) 1 small shallot, minced 1 cut low-sodium chicken broth 1/8 teaspoon ground pepper 2 tablespoons water 1 tablespoon cornstarch Remove and discard skin and visible fat from chicken breasts. In large skillet over medium heat, melt margarine. Add chicken, cook 10 to 15 minutes, turning until browned on all sides. Remove chicken; drain on paper towels. Add carrot, celery, green pepper, and shallot; cook stirring constantly, 2 minutes. Remove vegetables; set aside. Stir in broth and pepper; add chicken. Reduce heat to low; cover and simmer 15 minutes or until chicken is cooked through. Remove breasts to serving plate; keep warm. In cup, stir together water and cornstarch until smooth; stir into skillet. Over medium heat, bring to boil; boil 1 minute, stirring constantly. Stir in vegetables ; cook until heated through. To serve, spoon vegetables over chicken. Nutritional Figures Per Serving

Calories 380. Protein 62 grams. Carbohydrate 9 grams. Fat 9 grams. Cholesterol 152 mg. Sodium 201 mg.

CHICKEN STROGANOFFServes 4 This is a 1990s version of a nineteenth-century Russian classic. By substituting plain, lowfat yogurt for sour cream, you're decreasing the calories in this recipe by 332 calories. 4 skinless, boneless chicken breast halves or 1 thin sliced boneless roaster breast 2 tablespoons vegetable oil, divided 2 medium onions, thinly sliced 1/2 pound mushrooms, thinly sliced (2 cups) 1 clove garlic, minced 1/2 cup low sodium chicken broth 1/8 teaspoon ground pepper 2 tablespoons water 1 tablespoon cornstarch 1 container (8-ounces) plain low-fat yogurt hot cooked noodles, cooked without salt Remove and discard visible fat from chicken; slice chicken in thin strips. In large skillet over medium heat, heat 1 tablespoon oil. Add onions; cook 2 minutes, stirring frequently. Add mushrooms; cook 3 minutes longer. Remove vegetables from skillet; set aside. Heat remaining oil in skillet. Add chicken and garlic; cook 3 minutes or until chicken turns white, stirring frequently. Return vegetables to skillet; add broth and pepper.

In cup, blend water and cornstarch; stir into skillet. Over medium heat, bring to a boil; boil 1 minute, stirring constantly. Remove from heat; stir in yogurt until well blended. Heat gently over low heat (do not boil). Serve over noodles.

Nutritional Figures Per Serving Calories 427. Protein 65 grams. Carbohydrate 13 grams. Fat 12 grams. Cholesterol 155 mg. Sodium 182 mg.

CITRUS-MARINATED CHICKEN WINGSServes 3 Taste tests show that the parts of the bird that get the most exercise, such as the wings, leg, and neck have the deepest flavor. The seasonings in this recipe bring out the wonderful flavor of wings. 10 chicken wings 3 tablespoons vegetable oil grated peel and juice of 1 lemon grated peel and juice of 1 orange 2 cloves garlic, minced 6 whole cloves 2 bay leaves Fold wing tips back to form triangles. Place wings in shallow baking pan. In small saucepan, stir together remaining ingredients and heat over medium heat 5 minutes. Pour mixture over wings. Cover; refrigerate several hours or overnight. Preheat oven to 400oF. Bake wings 30 minutes or until tender, basting occasionally.

Nutritional Figures Per Serving Calories 137. Protein 9 grams. Carbohydrate 2 grams. Fat 10 grams. Cholesterol 25 mg. Sodium 24 mg.

ROASTER BREAST A L'ORANGE Serves 6 If you have a choice when buying the orange for this recipe, buy a Valencia in preference to a Navel. Navel oranges are excellent eating oranges, but they're not good juice oranges; the juice develops an off flavor if not used within half an hour. The Valencia, on the other hand, has a more stable flavor in its juice form. 1 roaster breast 1-1/2 tablespoons cornstarch 1-1/2 tablespoons firmly packed brown sugar Dash ground pepper 2/3 cup orange juice 2/3 cup low-sodium chicken broth 1/4 cup julienne-cut orange peel strips 1 tablespoon fresh lemon juice Preheat oven to 350oF. Place breast skin-side up in roasting pan; roast 45 minutes. Meanwhile, in 2-quart saucepan, stir together cornstarch, sugar and pepper. Gradually stir in orange juice and broth until smooth. Over medium heat, bring to a boil; boil 1 minute, stirring constantly. Remove from heat. Stir in orange peel and lemon juice. Roast chicken, basting frequently with sauce for 20 minutes longer or until juices run clear with no hint of pink when a cut is made near the bone. Heat remaining sauce and serve with roaster breast.

Nutritional Figures Per Serving Calories 168. Protein 20 grams. Carbohydrate 9 grams. Fat 5 grams. Cholesterol 54 mg. Sodium 54 mg.

CORNISH HENS WITH MUSHROOMS Serves 4 Skim milk contains all the calcium and protein of whole milk. Use it to make a prudent version of mushroom "cream" sauce. 2 fresh Cornish game hens 3 tablespoons vegetable oil 1/2 pound mushrooms, halved or quartered 2 small onions, peeled and cut in thin wedges 1 cup low-sodium chicken broth 1/8 teaspoon ground pepper 2 bay leaves 1 cup skim milk 1 tablespoon cornstarch Remove and discard any fat from cavities of hens. In a 5- quart Dutch oven or large deep skillet, over medium heat, heat oil. Add hens; cook about 20 minutes, turning to brown on all sides. Remove hens from pan and set aside. Pour off all but 2 tablespoons drippings; stir in mushrooms and onion. Cook 3 minutes or until tender, stirring occasionally. Stir in broth, pepper and bay leaves. Return hens to pan; reduce heat to medium low. Cover and simmer 45 minutes or until tender. Remove hens to serving platter and cut in half. Discard bay leaves. In cup, blend milk and cornstarch until smooth; stir into liquid in pan. Over medium heat, bring to a boil; boil 1 minute, stirring constantly. Serve sauce with hens.

Nutritional Figures Per Serving Calories 446. Protein 38 grams. Carbohydrate 9 grams. Fat 28 grams. Cholesterol 111 mg. Sodium 151 mg.

CORNISH HENS WITH APPLE STUFFING

Serves 4 Microwave Recipe

No extra cooking time is needed when you stuff fresh Cornish game hens before microwaving. 2 fresh Cornish game hens 3 tablespoons unsalted margarine, divided 1 tart red apple, coarsely chopped 1/4 cup chopped celery 1/4 cup chopped onion 1 cup fresh whole-wheat bread cubes (2 slices) 1/2 teaspoon poultry seasoning 1/8 teaspoon ground pepper 2 tablespoons cider or apple juice divided 1/4 teaspoon paprika Remove and discard any fat from cavities of hens. Place 2 tablespoons margarine in a 4 cup glass container; microwave at HIGH (100% power) 45 seconds. Add apple, celery and onion; cover with plastic wrap. Microwave at HIGH (100% power) 3 minutes, stirring once. Stir in bread cubes, poultry seasoning, pepper and 1 tablespoon cider. Spoon stuffing mixture lightly into cavities and close openings with toothpicks. Arrange hens, with legs pointing toward center, on microwave-safe roasting utensil. Place remaining 1 tablespoon margarine in custard cup; microwave at HIGH 25 seconds. Stir in remaining 1 tablespoon cider and paprika; brush mixture on hens. Cover hens with wax paper. Microwave at MEDIUM HIGH (70% power) 10 minutes per pound (combined weight of both hens). Let stand, covered, 10 minutes. To serve, cut hens in half.

Nutritional Figures Per Serving Calories 436. Protein 35 grams. Carbohydrate 13 grams. Fat 26 grams. Cholesterol 110 mg. Sodium 170 mg.

CURRIED ROASTER DRUMSTICKS

Serves 4

In this recipe, you'll see vegetable oil instead of butter or margarine or lard. Solid fats contain saturated fat, either because they came from animal sources (butter or lard) or because they have been hydrogenated (shortening or margarine).

5 roaster drumsticks
2 tablespoons vegetable oil
2 medium apples (diced 2 cups)
3/4 cup chopped onion
1 clove garlic, minced
1 tablespoon curry powder
1 teaspoon ground ginger
1/4 teaspoon ground pepper
1-1/2 cups low-sodium chicken broth
3 tablespoons cold water
1-1/2 tablespoons cornstarch

Remove and discard skin and visible fat from drumsticks. In large skillet over medium-high heat, heat oil. Add drumsticks; cook about 15 minutes, turning until browned on all sides. Remove; drain on paper towels. Pour off all but 1 tablespoon fat. Add apple, onion, garlic, curry, ginger and pepper; cook 2 to 3 minutes, stirring frequently. Stir in broth. Return chicken to skillet; reduce heat to medium low. Simmer, uncovered, stirring occasionally for 40 minutes or until chicken is tender and cooked through. Remove chicken to platter; keep warm. In cup, blend water and cornstarch until smooth; stir into skillet. Over medium heat, bring to boil; boil 1 minute, stirring occasionally. Spoon sauce over chicken.

Nutritional Figures Per Serving Calories 207. Protein 17 grams. Carbohydrate 15 grams. Fat 9 grams. Cholesterol 51 mg. Sodium 74 mg.

GREEK LEMON CHICKEN

Serves 4

This recipe adapts well to barbecuing.

1 chicken (3 pounds), quartered
1/2 cup fresh lemon juice (about 2 lemons)
2 tablespoons cold pressed (extra virgin) olive oil
1 medium-sized onion, sliced into thin rings
2 tablespoons minced fresh oregano or 2 teaspoons dried
2 teaspoons minced fresh thyme or 1/2 teaspoon dried
1/4 teaspoon ground black pepper
Cayenne pepper to taste (optional)
Lemon wedges, fresh oregano and thyme leaves (optional garnish)

Remove and discard visible fat from chicken. In large, shallow bowl, combine remaining ingredients except garnishes. Add chicken and marinate in refrigerator 30 minutes or longer. Preheat broiler. Drain chicken from marinade; place on rack in broiler pan. Broil chicken quarters, 4 inches from heat, for 30 to 35 minutes or until cooked through, turning and basting with marinade 3 to 4 times during cooking. Add onion rings during last 10 minutes of broiling time. Serve chicken with onion slices and garnish with lemon wedges, and sprigs of fresh oregano and thyme, if desired.

Nutritional figures per serving Calories 389. Protein 38. Carbohydrate 5 grams. Fat 24 grams. Cholesterol 122 mg. Sodium 110 mg.

LEMON DRUMSTICKS AND THIGHSServes 4 Both the grill and the broiler are good friends to the dieter because any fat that cooks out of your chicken just drops away into the fire or pan below. The juice and rind from lemons help achieve tasty, no salt basting. 4 chicken drumsticks 4 chicken thighs 1/3 cup lemon juice 3 tablespoons water 2 tablespoons vegetable oil 1 tablespoon finely shredded lemon peel 1 clove garlic, minced 1/4 teaspoon salt (or less) 1/8 teaspoon ground pepper Remove and discard skin and visible fat from drumsticks and thighs. Place in large, shallow dish. In small bowl, stir together lemon juice, water, oil, lemon peel, garlic, salt and pepper; pour over chicken. Cover; refrigerate several hours or overnight, turning occasionally. Prepare outdoor grill for cooking or preheat broiler. Remove from marinade. Grill 6 inches from source of heat or broil indoors, cooking about 30 to 40 minutes or until tender and golden brown; turn and baste frequently with marinade.

Nutritional Figures Per Serving Calories 220. Protein 26 grams. Carbohydrate 2 grams. Fat 12 grams. Cholesterol 80 mg. Sodium 217 mg.

ORIENTAL CHICKEN AND VEGETABLESServes 4 Fresh garlic is definitely better than powdered garlic. If you haven't been using it, give fresh garlic a try. Look for garlic cloves with plump, firm heads that have a fresh appearance. The paper-like casing should be dry and should completely cover the individual garlic cloves, and there should be no trace of sprouting. Store garlic in a cool, dry place, but don't refrigerate it. I asked a garlic grower why not, and he told me that cool temperatures can increase the garlic's tendency to sprout. 4 roaster boneless thigh cutlets 2 tablespoons cornstarch Ground pepper to taste 1 cup low-sodium chicken broth at room temperature 1 tablespoon reduced-sodium soy sauce 2 tablespoons vegetable oil 2 tablespoons sliced scallions 1 clove garlic, minced 1 cup diagonally sliced carrots (about 2 medium) 1 cup snow peas 1 cup well-drained bean sprouts 1 can (8-ounces) sliced water chestnuts, drained hot cooked rice (cooked without salt) Trim visible fat from thighs; cut chicken in thin strips. In small bowl, stir together cornstarch and pepper. Gradually stir in broth and soy sauce until smooth; set aside. In wok or large skillet over medium-high heat, heat oil. Add green onions and garlic; stir-fry 30 seconds. Add chicken and carrots; stir-fry 3 to 5 minutes or until chicken turns white and carrots are tender crisp. Add snow peas, bean sprouts and water chestnuts. Stir-fry to heat through. Re-stir cornstarch mixture; add to wok. Over medium heat, bring to a boil; boil l minute, stirring constantly. Serve over rice.

Nutritional Figures Per Serving Calories 304. Protein 28 grams. Carbohydrate 17 grams. Fat 13 grams. Cholesterol 73 mg. Sodium 268 mg.

PASTA PRIMAVERA WITH CHICKENServes 6 Because freshly grated Parmesan cheese has a more intense flavor than pre-grated cheese, you can use less of it, and in the process, you'll be saving on both fat and calories. When I'm cooking pasta for Frank, I omit both the oil and salt called for in the directions on the pasta package. If we're having guests, though, I use the salt and oil called for in the package directions; people who aren't used to low-fat, low-salt cooking would find it pretty bland otherwise. 4 skinless, boneless chicken breast halves or 1 thin sliced boneless roaster breast 2 tablespoons vegetable oil, divided 4 scallions, cut in julienne strips (about 1/2 cup) 2 cloves garlic, minced 1 pound asparagus, peeled, cut in 2-inch pieces or julienne zucchini (about 2 cups) 2 carrots, peeled, cut in julienne strips (about 1 cup) 1/2 cup low-sodium chicken broth 1/2 cup dry white wine 1/4 cup minced fresh parsley 1 1/2 teaspoons minced, fresh oregano, or 1/2 teaspoon dried 1/8 teaspoon ground pepper 1/2 pound spaghetti, cooked, drained 1/3 cup freshly grated Parmesan cheese Slice breast meat into thin strips. In a large skillet, over medium-high heat, heat 1 tablespoon oil. Add scallions and garlic; cook 1 minute, stirring frequently. Add chicken; cook 2 to 3 minutes or until chicken turns white, stirring constantly. Remove chicken and vegetables; set aside. Heat remaining oil in skillet; add asparagus and carrots and cook 2 minutes, stirring frequently. Stir in broth, wine, parsley, oregano and pepper; simmer 1 to 2 minutes or until vegetables are tender crisp. Place spaghetti on large platter; top with chicken mixture. Sprinkle with cheese. Toss and serve.

Nutritional Figures Per Serving Calories 417. Protein 48 grams. Carbohydrate 34 grams. Fat 9 grams. Cholesterol 105 mg. Sodium 185 mg. PINEAPPLE-MINTED ROASTERServes 8 Microwave Recipe Fat attracts more microwave energy than muscle does. That's good for you if you're on a low-fat diet because when you microwave chicken, the fat will render out into the drippings where you can easily discard it. 1 whole roaster (about 6 pounds) 1 can (20-ounces) pineapple chunks in their own juice about 1/2 cup pineapple juice, orange juice, or water 1-1/2 tablespoons cornstarch 5-6 small sprigs fresh mint or 1-1/2 teaspoons dried mint leaves 2 tablespoons unsalted margarine, melted Remove and discard any visible fat from roaster cavity. Remove giblets. Place, breast side down, on microwave-safe roasting utensil. Drain pineapple chunks, reserving juice and chunks. Add additional juice or water to reserved juice to measure 1-1/2 cups. Place cornstarch in 4-cup glass container and gradually stir juice into cornstarch until smooth. Microwave at HIGH (100% power) 2 minutes; stir and microwave 2 minutes longer or until mixture boils and thickens. Add mint (if using fresh mint, remove sprigs after five minutes). Remove 1/2 cup of mixture for glaze; stir pineapple chunks into remaining mixture for sauce and set aside. Brush roaster with melted margarine; cover with wax paper. Microwave at MEDIUM-HIGH (70% power) 10 to 12 minutes per pound, brushing with glaze several times during cooking. Halfway through cooking time, turn roaster over, using paper towels to protect hands. Pour off drippings and reserve, if desired. Baste bird with glaze and cover again with wax paper; complete cooking. Let stand, covered with aluminum foil, 20 minutes. (Standing time is important even if Bird-Watcher Thermometer has popped.) After standing time, juice should run clear with no hint of pink when thigh is pierced. To reheat sauce, microwave at HIGH for two minutes. Serve hot sauce with roaster.

Nutritional Figures Per Serving: Calories 343. Protein 38 grams. Carbohydrate 14 grams. Fat 14 grams. Cholesterol 107 mg. Sodium 97 mg. ROASTED CORNISH HENS WITH NEW POTATOESServes 4 When you combine tender-skinned new potatoes with Cornish game hens, you have almost a complete meal in one pan. Add a fresh green vegetable to complete a wholesome menu. 2 fresh Cornish game hens vegetable cooking spray 2 tablespoons unsalted margarine, melted 1 teaspoon minced shallot or scallion 1 and 1/2 teaspoons fresh rosemary or 1/2 teaspoon dried ground pepper to taste 6 small new potatoes, quartered 16 pearl onions, peeled 1 cup low-sodium chicken broth 2 tablespoons cold water 1 tablespoon cornstarch Preheat oven to 350oF. With sharp knife or poultry shears, cut hens lengthwise in half. Remove and discard any visible fat from cavity. Spray shallow roasting pan lightly with vegetable cooking spray. Place hens skin-side up in pan. Stir together margarine and shallot; brush on hens and sprinkle with rosemary and pepper. Arrange potatoes and onions around hens. Cover pan with foil. Bake 20 minutes. Uncover and continue baking, basting occasionally, 20 to 30 minutes or until hens and vegetables are tender. Remove to serving platter. Cover with foil; keep warm. Pour pan drippings into measuring cup. Allow to stand several minutes until fat drippings separate from hen juices; discard fat. Return hen juices to roasting pan; add broth. Bring to a boil over medium heat, stirring up brown bits from bottom of pan. In cup, blend water and cornstarch until smooth; stir into broth mixture. Bring to a boil; boil 1 minute, stirring constantly. Serve gravy with hens and vegetables. Nutritional Figures Per Serving Calories 463. Protein 38 grams. Carbohydrate 25 grams. Fat 23 grams. Cholesterol 110 mg. Sodium 129 mg.

ROASTER PAPRIKASHServes 8 This comment has nothing to do with this recipe, but I'm slipping it in here because I thought you might like to know about it! Fitness declines if you exercise two days or less each week. Fitness is maintained if you exercise three days a week. Fitness is improved if you exercise four or more days a week. 1 whole roaster (about 6 pounds) 1/4 cup vegetable oil 8 small white onions, peeled 4 carrots, peeled and quartered 1-1/4 cups low-sodium chicken broth 2 tablespoons paprika, divided 1/4 teaspoon ground pepper 1/4 cup water 2 tablespoons cornstarch 1 cup plain low-fat yogurt Remove and discard any visible fat from cavity. Remove giblets, tie legs together and fold wings back. Fasten neck with wooden pick or small skewer. In 8-quart saucepot over medium heat, heat oil. Add roaster. Cook about 30 minutes, turning until browned on all sides. Remove and set aside. Add onions and carrots; cook 3 minutes, stirring frequently. Remove vegetables. Pour off fat and stir in broth, 1 tablespoon paprika and pepper. Return roaster to saucepot; sprinkle with remaining paprika. Arrange onions and carrots around roaster. Reduce heat to medium low; cover and simmer 1 hour or until roaster juices run clear with no hint of pink when thigh is pierced and vegetables are tender. Remove roaster and vegetables to serving platter; keep warm. In cup, blend water and cornstarch until smooth; stir into liquid in saucepot. Bring to a boil over medium heat; boil 1 minute, stirring constantly. Remove from heat; add yogurt and stir until well blended and smooth. Heat gently over low heat; do not boil. Serve sauce with roaster and vegetables.

Nutritional Figures Per Serving Calories 387. Protein 41 grams. Carbohydrate 12 grams. Fat 19 grams. Cholesterol 109 mg. Sodium 142 mg.

TANDOORI CORNISH HENSServes 4 Fresh Cornish game hens contain even less fat and fewer calories than larger poultry and are close in size and flavor to the chickens traditionally used for India's Tandoori Chicken. If you want a barbecue version of this, using chicken breasts, look for "Boneless Breasts Tandoori" in Chapter Five. 2 fresh Cornish game hens 1/3 cup plain yogurt 2 tablespoons vegetable oil 2 tablespoons lime juice 1 tablespoon curry powder 2 cloves garlic, minced 2 teaspoons minced fresh gingerroot 1 teaspoon grated lime peel 1 teaspoon chili powder 1 teaspoon paprika With sharp knife or poultry shears, cut hens lengthwise in half. Remove and discard any visible fat from cavities. Place hens in large shallow baking dish. In small bowl, stir together remaining ingredients; brush on all sides of hens. Cover; refrigerate several hours or overnight to marinate. Preheat oven to 400oF. Place hens on rack in shallow baking pan; brush with marinade. Bake 15 minutes. Reduce oven temperature to 350oF; bake 20 to 25 minutes longer or until chicken is tender and juices run clear with no hint of pink when thigh is pierced with a fork.

Nutritional Figures Per Serving: Calories 384. Protein 36 grams. Carbohydrate 4 grams. Fat 24 grams. Cholesterol 111 mg. Sodium 124 mg.

TARRAGON ROASTED CHICKENServes 4 Make a light, clear pan gravy for chicken by removing fat from drippings and using cornstarch instead of flour to thicken; 1 tablespoon cornstarch = 2 tablespoons flour. 1 whole chicken (about 3 pounds) 3 tablespoons unsalted margarine 1 tablespoon minced fresh tarragon or 1-1/2 teaspoons dried 1/8 teaspoon ground pepper 4 sprigs fresh parsley 2 cloves garlic, peeled 1 cup low-sodium chicken broth 2 tablespoons dry white wine 1 tablespoon cornstarch Remove and discard any visible fat from cavity of chicken. Remove giblets. Preheat oven to 350oF. In small saucepan, over medium heat, melt margarine; stir in tarragon and pepper. Place parsley and garlic in cavity of chicken; tie legs together. Place chicken, breast-side up, in roasting pan; brush with tarragon mixture. Roast, brushing occasionally with remaining tarragon mixture, for about 1 1/2 hours or until juices run clear with no hint of pink when thigh is pierced. Remove chicken to serving platter; keep warm. Pour pan drippings into measuring cup. Allow to stand several minutes until clear fat drippings separate from chicken juices; discard fat drippings. Return chicken juices to roasting pan; add broth. In cup, blend wine and cornstarch; stir into roasting pan. Over medium heat, bring to a boil, stirring up brown bits from bottom of pan; boil 1 minute. Serve gravy with chicken.

Nutritional Figures Per Serving Calories 407. Protein 39 grams. Carbohydrate 3 grams. Fat 25 grams. Cholesterol 122 mg. Sodium 124 mg.

THYME THIGHSServes 4 Wine is a flavor bargain, if you're counting calories. The alcohol calories in this recipe will evaporate away, but the flavor of the wine remains. 6 chicken thighs 2 tablespoons flour 1/8 teaspoon ground nutmeg 1/8 teaspoon Cayenne pepper 2 tablespoons vegetable oil 1 tablespoon fresh, minced thyme or 1 teaspoon dried 1/2 cup dry white wine Remove skin from thighs and trim visible fat. On wax paper, combine flour, nutmeg, and pepper. Coat thighs with flour mixture. Heat oil in large skillet over medium-high heat. Add thighs and cook 10 to 15 minutes or until lightly browned, turning once. Sprinkle thyme on chicken and pour wine on top. Cover, reduce heat to medium low and cook 30 minutes or until chicken is tender.

Nutritional Figures Per Serving Calories 235. Protein 24 grams. Carbohydrate 4 grams. Fat 13 grams. Cholesterol 71 mg. Sodium 66 mg.

CRUNCHY BAKED DRUMSTICKS Serves 4 The grated lemon peel and the pepper can minimize the need for salt in this recipe. If you're on a low salt diet, skip the salt. 6 chicken drumsticks 1 egg white, lightly beaten 2 tablespoons lowfat milk 1/2 teaspoon salt or to taste 1/4 teaspoon ground pepper 1 cup crunchy nut-like cereal nuggets or bran flakes, crushed (Grapenuts) 1 teaspoon grated lemon peel Vegetable cooking spray

Preheat oven to 350oF. In shallow bowl, beat together egg white, milk, salt and pepper. On waxed paper, combine cereal and lemon peel. Roll drumsticks evenly in egg white mixture, then in cereal mixture, turning to coat well.

Spray a rectangular baking dish or cookie sheet with vegetable cooking spray. arrange drumsticks in dish in a single layer. Bake 50 to 60 minutes or until cooked through and golden.

Nutrition Figures per Serving Calories 294. Protein 26 grams. Fat 10 grams. Carbohydrate 25 grams. Sodium 535 mg. Cholesterol 74.

CAPE COD CHICKEN BREASTS Serves 4 The cranberries called for in this recipe are available in your supermarket produce section from September through November. If you want to have cranberries available for use at another time of the year, buy them when they're available and then freeze them in the bag they came in, but enclose that bag in a freezer bag so the berries are double wrapped. They'll stay in good condition for about nine months. 4 chicken breast halves ground pepper to taste 1 to 2 tablespoons vegetable oil or margarine 1 medium onion, finely chopped 1-1/2 cups fresh or frozen, thawed cranberries 3/4 cup orange juice 2 to 3 tablespoons sugar 1 teaspoon grated fresh orange peel pinch nutmeg

Removed skin, and season chicken on both sides with pepper. In a large skillet, over medium-high heat, heat oil. Add chicken breasts and cook for 4 to 5 minutes per side until golden brown. Add onion; cook 2 minutes longer, stirring often. Add cranberries, orange juice, sugar, orange peel and nutmeg. Stir to scrape up bits from bottom of skillet; bring to a boil. Reduce heat to medium-low; cover and cook 20 to 25 minutes longer or until chicken is tender and cranberries are soft, stirring occasionally. Remove chicken to warm platter; keep warm. Transfer cranberry mixture from skillet to food processor or blender; cover and puree until almost smooth. To serve, pour sauce over chicken.

Nutrition Figures per Serving Calories 514. Protein 48 grams. Fat 26 grams. Carbohydrate 20 grams. Sodium 144 mg. Cholesterol 145 mg.

MEDITERRANEAN CHICKEN BREASTSServes 4 Fresh garlic, stored in a cool, dry place will last about as long as a fresh onion. If the cloves start to sprout, you can still use them, but they won't be quite as flavorful. 4 chicken breast halves 1 to 2 tablespoons olive oil ground pepper to taste 1/2 cup dry red wine 4 fresh or canned plum tomatoes, seeded and coarsely chopped 2 garlic cloves, minced 1/2 teaspoon dried basil 1/2 teaspoon dried marjoram 1/2 cup pitted black olives, cut in half 1/4 cup minced, fresh parsley Remove skin from chicken breasts. In a large skillet, over medium heat, heat 1 tablespoon oil. Add chicken breasts and cook for 5 minutes until golden, turning once. Add more oil if necessary. Stir in wine, tomatoes, garlic, basil and marjoram; bring to a boil. Reduce heat to low; cover and simmer 20 to 25 minutes or until chicken is almost cooked through. Uncover; increase heat to medium- high and cook 5 minutes longer or until liquid is reduced by one-third. Stir in olives and parsley; heat through.

Nutrition Figures per Serving Calories 480. Protein 48 grams. Fat 30 grams. Carbohydrate 4 grams. Sodium 276 mg. Cholesterol 145 mg.

INDONESIAN CHICKEN KEBOBS WITH CURRIED YOGURT DIP Serves 4 You can use bottled lime juice in this recipe, but it lacks the spark that fresh lime juice has. Also, you can lower the sodium content still further by using light soy sauce. 2 tablespoons fresh lime juice 2 tablespoons soy sauce 1 tablespoon vegetable oil 1 teaspoon brown or white sugar 1 garlic clove, crushed 4 boneless, skinless chicken breast halves 1 cup plain lowfat yogurt 1/4 cup chopped scallions 1 tablespoon curry powder 1 teaspoon oriental sesame oil, optional

In a shallow bowl, combine lime juice, soy sauce, vegetable oil, sugar and garlic; mix well. Add chicken, turning to coat with marinade. Cover and refrigerate 1 hour.

Meanwhile, in small bowl, combine yogurt, scallions, curry powder and sesame oil. Cover and refrigerate until ready to use.

Remove chicken from marinade and cut into 3/4-inch cubes; reserve marinade. On each of 10 to 12 skewers, thread 4 to 5 chicken cubes. Preheat broiler. Place skewers in broiler pan; broil 4 inches from heat source 8 to 10 minutes until cooked through, turning once and brushing occasionally with marinade. Serve kebobs with curried yogurt dip.

Nutrition Figures per Serving Calories 234. Protein 35 grams. Fat 6 grams. Carbohydrate 8 grams. Sodium 645 grams. Cholesterol 82 mg.

POACHED CHICKEN IN CREAMY LEMON SAUCEServes 4 I'm fond of this recipe because the texture is creamy and it doesn't use cream. 4 boneless, skinless, chicken breast halves 1/4 teaspoon ground pepper 1/2 cup chicken broth 1/4 cup white wine 2 tablespoons lemon juice 1 teaspoon grated lemon peel 1 cup lowfat milk 1-1/2 tablespoons cornstarch 1 tablespoon Dijon mustard 2 tablespoons minced, fresh parsley, optional

Season chicken with pepper. In a large, deep skillet over medium-high heat, combine broth, wine, lemon juice and lemon peel; bring to a boil. Add chicken; reduce heat to medium-low. Cover and simmer 12 to 15 minutes or until chicken is cooked through. Transfer chicken to a warm serving plate and keep warm. In a small bowl, blend milk, cornstarch and mustard until smooth; stir into simmering liquid in skillet. Increase heat to medium; cook until mixture boils and thickens, stirring constantly. Return chicken to skillet; coat well with sauce. Sprinkle with parsley, if desired.

Nutrition Figures per Serving Calories 205. Protein 34 grams. Fat 4 grams. Carbohydrate 7 grams. Sodium 201 Cholesterol 84 mg.

CHICKEN AND BELL PEPPER SAUTEServes 4 This recipe is prettiest when made with red, green, and yellow bell peppers. However, your supermarket may not have the red and yellow ones available, in which case, substitute green ones. Incidentally, red bell peppers started out as green bell peppers, but as they matured, their color changed from green to red. 4 boneless, skinless chicken breast halves 1 teaspoon ground cumin 1 teaspoon dried oregano ground pepper to taste 1 to 2 tablespoons olive oil 1 clove garlic, minced 1 small red bell pepper, cut into thin strips 1 small green bell pepper, cut into thin strips 1 small yellow bell pepper, cut into thin strips

Place chicken breasts between sheets of plastic wrap and pound to 1/4 inch thickness. Sprinkle both sides of chicken with cumin, oregano and pepper to taste, pressing to make seasonings adhere.

In large skillet, over medium-high heat, heat oil. Add chicken; saute 1 to 2 minutes per side or until almost cooked through. Remove chicken to warm platter; keep warm.

Add garlic and pepper strips to drippings in skillet; stir- fry one minute. Reduce heat to medium-low; cover and cook 3 minutes or until peppers are tender-crisp. Return chicken to skillet, spooning pepper mixture on top. Cover and cook 3 to 5 minutes longer until vegetables are tender and chicken is completely cooked through.

Nutrition Figures per Serving Calories 209. Protein 32 grams. Fat 7 grams. Carbohydrate 3 grams. Sodium 91 grams. Cholesterol 79 mg.

CHICKEN NORMANDY Serves 4 If they're available, choose Rome Beauty apples for this recipe. Romes have a somewhat flat, mealy taste when eaten raw, but their flavor develops a wonderful richness when cooked. They're available from October until early Summer. The Golden Delicious, the Cortland, the Jonathan, and the Granny Smith are also good for baking. The Red Delicious apples, by the way, are only fair for cooking. 1 chicken, cut in serving pieces (about 3 pounds) Ground pepper to taste vegetable cooking spray 2 medium apples, cored and sliced 1 large onion, sliced 1/2 cup apple cider or juice 2 tablespoons fresh lemon juice 1 tablespoon vegetable oil 2 teaspoons brown sugar 1/4 teaspoon ground allspice

Preheat oven to 350F. Sprinkle chicken pieces with pepper to taste.

Spray 13 by 9-inch baking dish with vegetable cooking spray. Arrange chicken in baking dish; scatter apple and onion slices around and on top of chicken. In cup, combine cider, lemon juice, oil, sugar and allspice; pour over chicken. Bake, uncovered, for about 1 hour or until chicken is cooked through and apples are tender, turning pieces once during cooking and basting occasionally with drippings. To serve, remove chicken from pan juices and spoon apples and onions on top.

Nutrition Figures per Serving Calories 609. Protein 44 grams. Fat 39 grams. Carbohydrate 20 grams. Sodium 166 mg. Cholesterol 174 mg.

BALSAMIC CHICKEN AND MUSHROOMS Serves 4 If you can find balsamic vinegar, buy it! I've included red wine vinegar in case you can't find balsamic vinegar, but the balsamic vinegar is terrific in this recipe, and it's worth having on hand for salad dressings afterwards. 1 chicken, cut in serving pieces (about 3 pounds) Ground pepper to taste paprika 1-1/2 to 2 tablespoons olive oil, divided 2 tablespoons chopped shallots or scallions 2 cups sliced fresh mushrooms (about 1/2 pound) 1/2 cup chicken broth 2 tablespoons balsamic or red wine vinegar

Preheat oven to 350F. In large baking dish, place chicken, skin-side up; brush with 1/2 to 1 tablespoon oil and sprinkle with pepper and paprika to taste. Bake 40 minutes. Pour off and discard pan juices.

Meanwhile, in medium skillet over medium-high heat, heat remaining oil. Add shallots; saute 2 minutes until slightly softened. Stir in mushrooms; cook 2 minutes longer until lightly browned, stirring constantly. Add broth and vinegar; reduce heat to medium, and cook 3 minutes or until mushrooms are tender and liquid is slightly reduced. Pour mushroom mixture over chicken; bake 20 to 25 minutes longer until chicken is cooked through, basting occasionally with pan drippings. Serve chicken with mushroom sauce.

Nutrition Figures per Serving Calories 568. Protein 44 grams. Fat 41 grams. Carbohydrate 3 grams. Sodium 290 mg. Cholesterol 174 mg.

HARVEST CHICKEN DINNER Serves 8 Acorn squash is high in vitamin A. A single serving will more than meet your Recommended Daily Allowance for this vitamin. 1 whole roaster (about 6 pounds) 1/2 cup white wine 1/4 cup brown sugar 2 tablespoons cider vinegar 1 tablespoon vegetable oil 2 teaspoons dried rosemary leaves, crushed 1 teaspoon Worcestershire sauce 2 large acorn squash

Preheat oven to 350oF. Remove and discard and visible fat from roaster cavity. Remove giblets. Tie drumsticks together and fold wings back. Place chicken in roasting pan. In small bowl, combine wine, sugar, vinegar, oil, rosemary, Worcestershire; brush mixture on roaster, covering entire surface. Roast chicken 45 minutes.

Meanwhile, cut squash into quarters; remove seeds. After 45 minutes cooking time, arrange squash in roasting pan around chicken; fill cavities with a little rosemary mixture. Roast chicken, basting occasionally 1 1/4 to 1 3/4 hours longer (depending on weight) or until juices run clear with no hint of pink when thigh is pierced.

To serve, slice chicken with degreased pan juices and accompany with squash.

Nutrition Figures per Serving Calories 574. Protein 49 grams. Fat 31 grams. Carbohydrate 24 grams. Sodium 162 mg. Cholesterol 153 mg.

CAJUN SPICED ROASTER 8 If roasters aren't available in your area, you can use a regular whole chicken, adjusting the cooking time. However, roasters are juicier and tenderer and more flavorful, so if you've got a choice, go for a roaster. 1 whole roaster (about 6 pounds) 1 to 1-1/2 tablespoons dried thyme 2 teaspoons ground black pepper 1 teaspoon salt 1/2 to 1 teaspoon Cayenne pepper 1 clove garlic, minced 2 celery ribs, sliced (leaves included) 1 onion, quartered 1/4 cup parsley sprigs 1/2 lemon 1 tablespoon vegetable oil

Preheat oven to 350F. Remove and discard any visible fat from roaster cavity. Remove giblets. Rub roaster inside and out with lemon; brush oil evenly over skin.

In small bowl, combine thyme, black pepper, salt, red pepper, and garlic. Rub some of mixture into cavity of roaster; stuff with celery, onion and parsley. Skewer or tie cavity closed and fold back wings. Rub remaining herb and spice mixture evenly into skin of roaster, covering entire surface.

Place chicken in roasting pan. Roast 2 1/4 to 2 3/4 hours (depending on weight)or until juices run clear with no hint of pink when thigh is pierced. Baste occasionally with pan drippings.

To serve, remove celery, onion and parsley from cavity of roaster; discard. Skim fat from pan drippings and discard; reserve pan juices. Slice roaster and serve with pan juices. Nutrition Figures per Serving Calories 478. Protein 49 grams. Fat 29 grams. Carbohydrate 3 grams. Sodium 473. Cholesterol 153

Chapter Four—Chicken For Children

This chapter is going to be about cooking for and by kids, but I got the idea for it when I was thinking about something entirely different. I was idly wondering, "When is Frank the absolute happiest and most content?" Part of me instantly wanted to answer, "When working, of course." I believe that for him business is pleasure. If it's a busy time, he'll happily get along for weeks at a time on four hours sleep and work the rest except for meals. When it gets really busy, I've seen him get by on two hours—and still relish the work.

But there are certainly other things he enjoys. He's an avid baseball fan and the best Father's Day gift I think he ever got was tickets to go to one of the Oriole games with his son Jim and grandson Ryan. He also loves dancing (his nickname years ago used to be "twinkle toes").

Still, I think the time that he looks the most relaxed and content and generally pleased with life is when the four children and twelve grandchildren are here. They're scattered from Maine to Virginia, so we don't get them often, but when we do, it's an occasion. And it's one when I want to have food that I can count on the kids' liking.

Here are some of the principles of cooking for young children that I've learned from the Perdue home economists and from Cooperative Extension. I'm guessing that if you have kids, you know their preferences pretty well, but if you're entertaining other kids, these tips may come in handy.

_Finger foods such as chicken nuggets are always a hit. I keep a carton or two on hand for a never-fail snack food for kids$or grown-ups.

_Young children often prefer uncomplicated tastes. While some may go for elaborate sauces, it's safest to cook chicken by quickly sauteing it in your frying pan, and then have any of the grown-up's sauces available for the kids to use as an optional dip.

_Avoid highly seasoned foods for kids unless you know they're used to them.

_Frequently young children like uniform textures. Casseroles with hard and soft textures would be riskier than, say, a straightforward boned chicken breast.

_Pieces cut from a cooked Cornish hen can be a real treat for a small child. He or she eats the child-size portion, breast or leg, while the grown-ups eat regular size broiler breast or drumsticks.

_My friends in Cooperative Extension tell me that the latest scientific research suggests thinking of a balanced diet in terms of several days rather than just a rigid 24- hour period. That means that if one of the kids in your care goes on a chicken-eating jag or a peanut butter jag or a not-eating jag, don't worry; it's ok as long as in the course of several days he or she is getting a balanced diet. Knowing this can make meal time a lot more relaxed.

Cooking with school age kids can be a lot of fun, as long as it's presented as a treat instead of a chore. You might, for a start, get them involved in planning the week's menu. I know some families who allow each child to pick the main dish for one meal a week. Older children actually get to cook their choice. My daughter-in-law, Jan Perdue, suggests getting kids to pick out meals with an ethnic or international theme so that mealtime is a time to explore other cultures as well as a time to eat.

Many of the recipes in this chapter are not only popular with kids, they're designed to be easy and fun for them to make. When your kids are trying these recipes, how about teaching them some of the food preparation tips that will be useful to them for the rest of their lives?

When I'm cooking with kids, my first concern is food safety. I explain to them that in most cases food-borne illnesses don't make you violently sick (although they can); the usual episode is more likely to be simple queasiness or a headache or feeling under the weather and not knowing quite why. To avoid these nuisance illnesses as well as the possibility of more serious ones, the number one rule is:

_Wash your hands and all utensils before and after touching any raw meat.

Here are some other food preparation tips that kids should know:

_Before starting to cook, read the recipe carefully and gather all ingredients and equipment.

_Don't wear loose, floppy clothing or sleeves that are too long. Tie back hair if it gets in the way.

_When using a sharp knife, cut on a cutting board and point the knife away from your body.

_If you're walking around with a knife, hold it so the blade is pointed toward the floor and away from your body.

_Make sure you know how to light your stove. If a gas burner or oven doesn't light, turn the knob to "off" and ask an adult for help. Electric burners remain hot even after they're turned off, so don't touch!

_When removing lids from cooking pots, point them away from you to prevent steam burns.

_Don't let pot handles extend over the edge of the stove or counter$a little brother or sister could grab the handle and pull it down on his or her head.

_Never stick anything into an electric mixer or blender while it's running.

_Don't let any part of your potholder touch the burner; it could catch fire.

_Clean up as you go along$and don't forget the cutting board.

_Double check that stove and appliances are turned off before you leave the kitchen. Make a habit of turning off the burner before removing your pan, that way you won't forget.

_Never be embarrassed to ask for help. That's how we learn.

Personally, I love having kids in the kitchen. I like the bustle and hubbub, and even though I know, as I'm sure you do too, that we parents could probably do things a lot faster without their "help," that's not the point. The point is being together and doing things together and having fun together.

ALLISON'S CHIX IN A BLANKET

At age 8, our granddaughter Allison Perdue, loves to make these. She tells me that her 6-year old brother can make them too. She got the recipe from summer camp, but changed the main ingredient to Frank's franks. If you can't find Frank's franks, use any chicken hot dog. It will have much less fat than regular franks. I've watched Ally make these, and sometimes the biscuits stay wrapped around the frank, and sometimes they open during cooking. Ally says they're okay either way. 2 biscuits from a tube of buttermilk refrigerator biscuits, uncooked 1 chicken frank 1 tablespoon of grated cheddar cheese, or more, to taste Lay the biscuits side by side with the sides touching. Pinch together the parts that are touching and then, using your palms or a rolling pin, press or roll the biscuits into a single rectangle that's hot dog shaped, only wider. Lay a frank on the dough and then sprinkle the frank with the cheese. Pierce frank in several places with fork. Wrap the dough around the frank, pinch closed, and then bake according to the directions for cooking the biscuits. BBQ "SPARERIBS" Makes 40, Serves 8-10 One of my favorite commercials is of Frank introducing the Perdue Chicken Franks. It starts out with Frank in front of a hot dog stand calling out, "Hot dogs only 25 cents." A young kid who's been made up to have a large nose and ears just like Frank's, says, "Only 25 cents for a hot dog? How good could it be?" Frank answers, "I'm making it easy for people to try Perdue Chicken Franks." The kid answers, "Chicken Franks? Free would be a lot easier." When Frank answers that his franks cost less and have 25% less fat, the kid answers, "All right, I'll bite," and then says, "Tastes as good a real hot dog." Frank looks at the kid, with his Perdue-shaped nose and ears, and says, "This kid's got good taste and good looks."

These "spareribs" also taste good and look good. 8 chicken franks 1-1/4 cups prepared barbecue sauce 1 tablespoon finely chopped onion 1 teaspoon mustard Slice each frank on the diagonal into 5 pieces. In a large bowl, combine remaining ingredients. Add frank slices and toss gently to coat well. Arrange coated franks in single layer on baking sheet and place under broiler 2 minutes. Turn and broil 2 minutes longer, or until franks are golden brown. Watch carefully to avoid burning. Serve with toothpicks, if desired.

BETSY'S BEST-"GETTI" Serves 6-8 You can make this even simpler by using canned spaghetti. Also, if you top the casserole with thin slices of mozzarella and heat it until the mozzarella melts, you'll get a gloppy, stretchy, chewing-gum-like topping that kids will adore if they're into being messy. Mine love it. 8 chicken franks 1 pound spaghetti 3 tablespoons vegetable oil 1/2 cup finely chopped onion 1/2 clove garlic, minced 1 can (8-ounces) tomato sauce 1 can (16-ounces) whole tomatoes, chopped with liquid 1 1/2 teaspoons minced fresh basil or 1/2 teaspoon dried 1 tablespoon minced fresh parsley Grated Parmesan cheese Slice franks into thin rounds. In large kettle, over high heat, bring 3-1/2 quarts salted water to boil. Add spaghetti, stir and cook until tender. Drain and place in large bowl. In a medium saucepan over medium heat, heat oil. Add garlic and onion and cook for 3 minutes, stirring often. Add tomatoes and liquid, sauce and herbs. Stir and add franks. Bring to boil, reduce heat to medium-low and simmer 5 minutes. Pour sauce over spaghetti, toss to combine. Serve with Parmesan cheese. BIG TOP CORN DOGSServes 8 Because this involves deep fat frying, it's probably best cooked by adults or mature teenagers only, but the end result will impress your kids. 8 chicken franks 1/4 cup flour 1 package (8-ounces) corn muffin mix 2 eggs 1 cup milk vegetable oil for deep frying 8 wooden lollipop or caramel-apple sticks Pierce each frank in several places with a fork. Roll in flour and set aside. In a mixing bowl combine corn muffin mix, eggs and milk; mix thoroughly. In large fryer or

deep, heavy skillet, heat 1 1/2 inches of vegetable oil to 375oF or until bread cube sizzles in it. Dip each frank in batter, coating evenly. Place gently into oil; cook 3-4 at one time, turning until golden brown all over. Drain on paper towels. Place corn dogs on lightly-oiled shallow baking sheet and bake at 375oF for 8 minutes or until thoroughly heated. Insert stick at least 2-inches into corn dog. Serve with mustard and ketchup.
CHICKEN DIVANServes 4-6 This is an easy recipe for a kid when he or she is in charge of making dinner for the family. 1 package (10-ounces) frozen broccoli, uncooked 2 packages fully cooked chicken breast tenders 1/2 teaspoon salt or to taste 1 can (10-1/2-ounces) cream of celery soup, undiluted 1 cup shredded Cheddar cheese Preheat oven to 400oF. Place broccoli across bottom of baking dish; sprinkle with salt. Arrange chicken tenders in a layer on top of broccoli. Pour soup over chicken. Sprinkle with cheese. Bake, uncovered for 20-30 minutes or until broccoli is just tender.
CHICKEN PIZZAS Serves 3 If you want something unusual for the teenagers, this is it. It's tasty and not much trouble. 6 chicken drumsticks 1 can (10-1/2-ounces) pizza sauce 1 cup grated Mozzarella cheese 1 package (10-ounces) refrigerated Parkerhouse rolls (unbaked) Preheat oven to 350oF. Pour pizza sauce in small bowl. Dip chicken in sauce; place on baking sheet. Bake, uncovered, for 45 minutes. Separate rolls and roll out one at a time to 5-inch circle. Dip chicken in pizza sauce again and roll in cheese. Place on round of dough; pull dough around chicken and pinch together. (Leave bony end of drumstick uncovered for finger eating.) Bake, uncovered, approximately 30 minutes longer or until dough is brown.
COZY KITTEN WHISKERSServes 16 A short cut for this is to use bread dough that comes in tubes in the refrigerator section of your supermarket. 16 chicken franks 1 package (13-3/4-ounces) hot roll mix butter or margarine Pierce each frank in several places with a fork. To make "whisker" on both ends of franks, lay frank on cutting board and make 4-lengthwise cuts 1-1/2-inches from each end. Cut carefully, rotating frank, so

that 8 "whiskers" result. Repeat with all franks. Prepare hot roll mix according to package directions. Or use the prepared bread dough that comes in tubes at the supermarket. Divide into 16 equal portions and roll each on lightly floured surface to 3 by 3-inch square. Starting at a corner, roll dough around middle of each frank, leaving ends of franks exposed. Place on buttered baking sheet, tucking dough tip under frank. Arrange "whiskers" fanned out. Brush with melted butter. Bake in preheated 375oF oven for 12 to 15 minutes until golden brown. Serve with mustard and ketchup in squeeze containers so children can "draw" faces.

CRISPY PEANUT BUTTER CHICKEN

Serves 4

I once heard a professor at the University of California at Davis argue that wine was the greatest cultural achievement of mankind. He's wrong, of course. It's really peanut butter. Or at least a lot of my young friends seem to think so. By the way, did you know that there are 540 peanuts in a 12-ounce jar of peanut butter? The first time I made this recipe, I skipped the 1/4 cup oil, just to see if I could save some calories. Having tried it, I don't recommend skipping any of the oil. It was too dry and crusty without it.

1 egg
1/2 cup peanut butter
1 teaspoon salt or to taste
1/2 teaspoon ground pepper
1/4 cup milk
3/4 cup bread crumbs
1 chicken, cut in serving pieces
1/4 cup oil

Preheat oven to 350oF. In a mixing bowl beat egg and peanut butter together; add salt and pepper. Add milk gradually, stirring well to blend. Place bread crumbs on a sheet of wax paper. Dip chicken in peanut butter mixture and roll in crumbs. Place chicken, skin side up, in single layer in shallow baking pan. Pour oil over chicken. Bake, uncovered, at 350oF for 1 hour, or until cooked through.

CROISSANT DOGS

Serves 6-8

I don't think I can count the number of times my son Carlos made this as a teenager. He's also served it to Frank. Carlos and I laugh over the idea of serving Frank's Franks to Frank.

8 chicken franks
1 package (8-ounces) crescent roll dough
2 tablespoons Dijon mustard
2 slices Swiss cheese, 7x4-inches
1 egg beaten with 1 tablespoon water
1-1/2 teaspoons poppy seeds (optional)

Preheat oven to

375°F. Pierce franks all over with tines of fork. Divide crescent rolls and place on lightly floured surface. Working with one piece of dough at a time, fold tips of long side of triangle in to meet at center. Then stretch triangle lightly up toward point. Cut cheese slices in half, then diagonally to form four triangular pieces. Brush dough with thin layer of mustard, top with cheese, brush with mustard again. Roll franks in the dough, starting at the bottom and rolling toward the point. Place on ungreased baking sheet so they are not touching. Brush lightly with egg wash and sprinkle with poppy seeds. Place in the middle of the oven for 15 to 20 minutes or until dough is golden brown.

CRUNCHY MINI DRUMSTICKS

Serves 4

Young children love miniature versions of adult food, but if you're serving this recipe to them, I recommend leaving out the Worcestershire sauce.

1/2 cup whole wheat flour
2 eggs, beaten
1 teaspoon Worcestershire sauce (optional)
3/4 teaspoon salt or to taste
1/4 teaspoon ground pepper
2 cups whole wheat or seasoned bread crumbs
2 tablespoons unsweetened wheat germ (optional)
1/3 cup vegetable oil
9 chicken wings
paprika

Preheat oven to 400°F. Place flour on wax paper. In shallow bowl, beat eggs with Worcestershire sauce, salt and pepper. On another sheet of wax paper, combine bread crumbs and wheat germ, if desired. Pour oil into a shallow roasting pan or large shallow baking dish and place in oven. With sharp knife, divide wings into 3 pieces, reserve bony wing tips to prepare chicken broth. Roll remaining "mini drumstick" pieces first in flour, then in egg mixture, and finally in bread crumbs. Sprinkle with paprika and arrange in preheated baking dish. Bake 10 minutes, then turn with tongs and bake 10 minutes longer. Reduce heat to 350°F; cook 10 to 15 minutes longer until crisp and golden brown. Drain on paper towels and serve warm or at room temperature.

DELI DOGS

Serves 6-8

Some teenagers love sauerkraut; some most definitely don't. This is a great dish for those who do.

8 chicken franks
1 can (16-ounces) sauerkraut
3 cups Bisquick
1 tablespoon caraway seeds
1/2 cup water
2 tablespoons prepared mustard (optional)
Flour
1 egg beaten with 1

tablespoon water Preheat oven to 375oF. Pierce franks all over with tines of fork. Drain sauerkraut thoroughly by pressing between two stacked dinner plates, then chop coarsely. In a large mixing bowl, combine Bisquick, sauerkraut and 2 teaspoons of the caraway seeds. Gradually add water and mix vigorously until soft, slightly sticky dough forms. Divide dough in half. Roll each half on a well-floured surface into a 7x16-inch rectangle approximately 1/4-inch thick. Cut each rectangle into four 7x4-inch pieces. Brush center of each piece of dough with a thin layer of mustard, if desired, then brush the outer 1/2-inch of the rectangle with egg wash. Roll each frank loosely a piece of dough. Tuck outer ends under and place seam-side down on lightly greased baking sheet so they are not touching. Brush lightly with egg wash and sprinkle with remaining caraway seeds. Bake in middle of oven for 30 minutes or until crust is golden brown. Serve with more mustard and relish if desired. JALAPENO BURGERSServes 4-6 This is good for older teenagers. Young kids ones may find the flavors too harsh. 1 package fresh ground chicken (about 1 pound) 2/3 cup shredded Monterey Jack cheese with jalapeno peppers 1/2 teaspoon cumin 1 teaspoon salt 8 taco shells 1 tomato, thinly sliced 1 avocado, thinly sliced 1 cup salsa Combine chicken and remaining seasonings. Form into 8 burgers. Grill or broil on lightly oiled surface 5 to 6- inches from heat source 4 to 5 minutes per side until burgers are cooked through. Serve in heated taco shells with slices of tomato and avocado. Top with salsa. MAPLE CRUNCH CHICKENServes 4 Maple syrup with chicken may seem a little unusual to you$but it's really good. Frank liked it so much that I've served it to him several times, once substituting boneless skinless chicken breasts. If you want to make that substitution, shorten the cooking time to about twenty minutes, or until a meat thermometer registers 170-175 degrees. Also, use instant oatmeal and toast it for a couple of minutes in the oven first, to compensate for the shorter time in the oven. 1 chicken, cut in serving pieces 1 egg 1/2 cup maple syrup 1/2 cup uncooked oatmeal 1 teaspoon salt or to taste 1/4 teaspoon ground pepper 1/3 cup oil Preheat oven to 350oF. In a shallow bowl beat egg with maple syrup. Place oatmeal, salt and pepper on a sheet of wax paper. Dip chicken pieces in egg mixture, then oatmeal mixture. Pour oil in shallow baking pan. Place chicken, skin side down, in oil in baking pan; turn chicken pieces to coat with oil; leave skin side up. Bake, uncovered, for approximately 1 hour, or until cooked through. NACHO NIBBLESServes 6 I've made this recipe scattering the cheese and franks and other ingredients over the tortilla chips haphazardly, and I've also made it so that each individual tortilla chip has its own slice of frank, its own chili and its own pepper and cheese. The second way looks more impressive. The first way is a lot easier. My son Jose likes to serve this at parties with his college friends. 8 chicken franks 1 package (16 ounces) tortilla chips 2 cups chili 2 scallions, thinly sliced 1/2 cup diced green pepper, or mild to hot green chili peppers 12 ounces grated Monterey Jack or Cheddar cheese Preheat oven to 350oF. Cut franks into thin slices. Place tortilla chips on large shallow baking pan and top with frank slices. Dab chili on top, then sprinkle with scallions, peppers and cheese. Bake nachos for 15 minutes or until cheese bubbles. PHOTO: Tucking chicken nuggets into pita pockets and arranging vegetables are easy steps in teaching children… - 5 NUGGETS IN A POCKETServes 4 This is an easy sandwich for teenagers to make. 1 package fully-cooked chicken breast nuggets 4 mini pita pockets prepared Thousand Island dressing or Magic Mixture Sauce (recipe follows) 1/2 cup shredded lettuce 8 cherry tomatoes, halved Bake nuggets following package directions. Slit top of pita pockets. Spoon 1 to 2 teaspoons sauce into each pocket and fill with nuggets, lettuce, tomato and additional sauce if desired. Serve with Rick Rack Carrot Sticks and Broccoli Trees (raw cut-up pieces of carrot and broccoli). Magic Mixture Sauce: In small bowl, combine 1/4 cup mayonnaise, 1/4 cup ketchup, 1 tablespoon prepared French dressing, 1/8 to 1/4 teaspoon curry powder (optional), and 1-2 drops Tabasco (optional). NUTTY BUDDY

CHICKEN

Serves 4

According to the Texas Peanut Producers' Board, we Americans eat 4 million pounds of peanuts each day. Tell your kids that, as they help you chop the salted peanuts for this recipe.

1 egg
2 tablespoons milk
1/3 cup all purpose flour
1 teaspoon salt or to taste
1/4 teaspoon ground pepper
1/3 cup bran buds
3/4 cup finely chopped salted peanuts
1 chicken, cut in serving pieces
1/2 cup melted butter or margarine

Preheat oven to 350oF. In a shallow bowl beat egg with milk. Place flour, salt, pepper, bran buds and peanuts on a sheet of wax paper and mix together. Dip chicken pieces in egg mixture; then flour mixture. Place chicken in single layer, skin side up, in shallow baking pan. Pour melted butter or margarine over chicken. Bake, uncovered, for about 1 hour or until cooked through.

PICNIC PACKET CHICKEN

Makes 4 packets

The whole picnic meal is ready to serve when these come out of the oven — and there are no portioning and serving problems. Children love this idea. You can also cook this on an outdoor grill.

1 chicken, cut in serving pieces
4 small raw carrots, cut in sticks
4 raw potatoes, quartered
1 teaspoon salt or to taste
1/4 teaspoon ground pepper
1/2 teaspoon dried oregano
4 teaspoons butter or margarine

Preheat oven to 350oF. Tear off 4 pieces heavy duty aluminum foil, approximately 18-inches square. Place 1 or 2 pieces of chicken on each piece of foil. Put one carrot and one potato on each piece of foil. Sprinkle salt, pepper and oregano over all. Add teaspoon of butter or margarine to each. Wrap tightly. Bake for approximately 1 hour or until chicken is cooked through.

POTATO CHIP DRUMSTICKS

Serves 4-6

These are wonderful for school lunch boxes. Since they're stored in the freezer, you can take them out a meal at a time and they'll defrost in the child's lunch box in time to eat later in the day.

6 chicken drumsticks
1/3 cup whole wheat flour
1 container (8-ounces) plain yogurt (1 cup)
salt and ground pepper to taste
1/4 teaspoon curry powder (optional)
1 package (7-ounces) no-salt potato chips, crushed

Preheat oven to 375oF. Grease a baking sheet. Remove skin from drumsticks. In small bowl, combine yogurt, salt, pepper and curry. On wax paper, place crushed potato chips. Roll drumsticks first in yogurt mixture and then in potato chips, pressing crumbs gently onto drumsticks to coat thoroughly. Arrange drumsticks on baking sheet and place in oven. Reduce heat to 350oF and bake 45 to 50 minutes until crisp and golden brown. Chill drumsticks, uncovered, on baking sheet. Then wrap individually in foil and freeze. If desired, allow extra foil at ends of package and twist to form a chicken. To pack for lunch: Freeze individual containers of juice overnight. Place frozen juice in lunch bag with well-chilled or frozen foil-wrapped drumsticks and fresh peas and cherry tomatoes in plastic bag. Frozen juice will keep other foods chilled and by lunchtime will be a "fruit slush" dessert. Variation: Instead of potato chips, use crushed salt-free tortilla chips and substitute chili powder for curry. PUNK PIZZA ROLLSServes 8 Tell your kids as they're eating this, "If you grew as fast as a chicken, you would have weighed 349 pounds by the time you were 2 months old!" 8 chicken franks 1 cup tomato sauce or pizza sauce 2 tablespoons finely chopped onion 1/2 teaspoon dried oregano 8 flour tortillas 1 1/2 cups shredded Mozzarella cheese Preheat oven to 350oF. Pierce each frank in several places with a fork. In a small bowl combine tomato sauce, onion, and oregano; spread equal amounts over each tortilla. Place one frank in center of each tortilla and roll up. Place rolls about one-inch apart in shallow baking dish and sprinkle each with equal amount of cheese. Bake for about 20 minutes or until cheese melts and bubbles. RAMAKI WRAPSMakes 64, Serves 16-18 This is a good appetizer for a teenage party. I've served it to kids who would never go for the chicken livers in the original ramaki recipe. They've loved this version, made with cut up franks. 8 chicken franks 1 can (8-ounces) water chestnuts, drained 32 strips bacon Preheat oven to 400oF. Cut each frank into 8 slices. Slice water chestnuts thinly. Halve bacon slices crosswise. For each ramaki, wrap frank slice and water chestnut slice with bacon; secure with toothpick. Place ramakis on a rack over large baking pan and bake for 15 minutes or until bacon is crisp.

RED EYE EGGROLLS
Makes 16, Serves 8

These take some work, but they've been a great success with both kids and adults. I've served them at parties where both have been present and the "egg rolls" vanished just about as fast as I could make them.

8 chicken franks
2 tablespoons vegetable oil
1 can (16-ounces) bean sprouts, drained
2 cups shredded Chinese cabbage or iceberg lettuce
1 tablespoon soy sauce
1/4 cup chicken broth
16 square eggroll wrappers (You might be able to find them in the produce section of your supermarket and they are available in Oriental food shops.)
1 egg, beaten
vegetable oil for deep frying

Halve franks crosswise, set aside. In large skillet, over medium-high heat, heat oil; add vegetables, toss and cook 2 minutes. Add soy sauce and broth. Reduce heat to medium-low and simmer, covered, 5 minutes; drain well in colander. Place eggroll wrapper on work surface with a corner pointing toward you; brush each corner with egg. Place two rounded tablespoons of vegetable mixture in center, then top with frank piece horizontally. Fold bottom corner over frank and filling, then fold right and left corners over and roll up to complete. In a wok, fryer or heavy skillet, heat 2-inches oil to 370°F or until a small cube of bread sizzles when placed in oil. Fry 3-4 eggrolls at a time until crisp all over. Drain well on paper towels. Before serving, re-heat on shallow baking pan in preheated 350°F oven for 10 to 12 minutes. (I don't recommend reheating them in the microwave. They'll come out soggy instead of crisp.)

SPICED CREAMED CONE CHICKEN
Serves 4

This is my first choice for when our twelve grandchildren are coming. The ice cream cone flavor is so subtle that no one has yet been able to identify it without being told. Still, the flavor is delicious.

1 teaspoon salt or to taste
1/4 teaspoon ground pepper
1/2 cup sour cream
1 tablespoon finely chopped onion
1/2 teaspoon ground allspice
8 ice cream cones, crushed (I use the sugar cones)
1 chicken, cut in serving pieces
2 tablespoons shortening

Preheat oven to 350°F. In a shallow bowl combine sour cream, salt, pepper, onion and allspice. Place cone crumbs on a sheet of wax paper. Dip chicken in sour cream mixture; then in cone crumbs. Melt shortening in shallow baking pan; place chicken in single layer, skin side up, in pan. Bake, uncovered, for about 1 hour or until cooked through.

SPICY SOUTHWESTERN CASSEROLE

Serves 6-8

Is there a teenage cook in the family? He or she could make this for the family dinner one night this week.

8 chicken franks
2 cans (15-ounces) chili
1 cup yellow cornmeal
2 teaspoons baking powder
1 teaspoon salt or to taste
2 eggs
2/3 cup melted butter or margarine
1 cup sour cream
1 can (16 ounces) niblets-style corn, drained
1/4 pound grated Monterey Jack or Cheddar cheese
1 can (4 ounces) chopped, mild green chilies, drained

Preheat oven to 375oF. Cut franks in half lengthwise. Place chili in bottom of a buttered 7x14x2-inch baking dish. Arrange franks, cut side down, on top of chili. In medium size mixing bowl, mix dry ingredients. Add eggs, butter, and sour cream and blend thoroughly. Fold in corn. Sprinkle half of the cheese and green chilies over the layer of franks. Top with half of the corn mixture. Sprinkle with remaining cheese and chilies and finish with a layer of corn mixture. Smooth the top with a spatula. Bake in the middle of oven for 35 to 40 minutes, or until top is lightly browned and toothpick inserted in corn layers comes out clean.

PHOTO: School's open, and crunchy Tater-Chip Drumsticks, fresh vegetables and frozen-juice "slush" earn high lunch bag... - 5

SWEET AND SOUR CHICKEN

Serves 4

This is one of the National Chicken Cooking Contest winners, and it's easy enough for the beginning cook. The original recipe called for adding a teaspoon of salt to the sweet and sour mixture, but I found that the salt in the salad dressing and the onion soup mix was enough. If your kids like foods salty, they may want to sprinkle more on at the end.

1 chicken, cut in serving pieces
1 bottle (8-ounces) Russian salad dressing
1 envelope (1-3/8-ounces) dry onion soup mix
1 jar (10-ounces) apricot preserves

Preheat oven to 350oF. Place chicken, skin side up, in single layer in large shallow baking dish. In a large measuring cup combine remaining ingredients and pour over chicken. Bake, uncovered, for about 1 hour, or until cooked through.

TACO DOGS
Serves 6-8

Our neighbors South of the Border might be surprised at this version of their tacos, but it's quick and good.

8 chicken franks
8 taco shells
1 can (15-ounces) chili with beans
1 cup shredded Monterey Jack or cheddar erey Jack or cheddar cheese
1 cup shredded lettuce
1/2 cup diced tomato

Preheat oven to 350F. Split franks in half lengthwise and grill or fry briefly. Place franks in taco shells and top each with 2 tablespoons chili and 1 tablespoon cheese. Place tacos on baking sheet and bake for 15 minutes, or until chili is hot and cheese is melted. Top with taco sauce, lettuce, tomato and remaining cheese. Serve immediately.

TATER FRANKS
Serves 6-8

This is inexpensive and easy to like.

8 chicken franks
3 tablespoons melted butter or margarine, divided
1-1/2 tablespoons milk
1 teaspoon salt or to taste
ground pepper to taste
3 cups cooked riced potatoes or very firm prepared instant mashed potatoes
2 egg yolks
2 egg whites, lightly beaten with 1 tablespoon water
2-1/2 cups cornflake crumbs

Preheat oven to 375oF. Pierce franks all over with a fork. Pour half of butter into a mixing bowl. Add milk, salt and pepper, then add riced potatoes and beaten egg yolks. (If using instant mashed potatoes, omit milk.) Beat thoroughly with wooden spoon until well blended; chill until firm enough to handle. Divide potato mixture into eight parts. Using your hands, form an even layer of potato (about 1/2- inch thick) around each frank. If mixture is sticky, flour hands lightly. Roll first in cornflake crumbs, then in egg white and water mixture, and again in crumbs. Place tater franks on buttered baking sheet so they are not touching, and drizzle with remaining melted butter. Bake in the middle of the oven for 30 minutes or until crisp and golden brown. Serve immediately.

TEAM SPIRIT HEROS
Serves 8

Your teenagers can make this one. If they don't like peppers or onions, it's fine to skip them.

8 chicken franks
8 hero rolls
4 tablespoons vegetable oil
1 onion, thinly sliced
2 green peppers, cut into thin strips
1-1/2 cups tomato sauce
1 tablespoon fresh, minced basil or 1

teaspoon dried 1 tablespoon minced fresh parsley 12 slices Provolone cheese, cut into half-inch strips Pierce each frank in several places with a fork. Cut rolls lengthwise, leaving the two halves attached. In a large skillet over medium-low heat, heat oil. Add onions and peppers and cook for 10 minutes stirring often. Add sauce and herbs; stir and simmer 5 minutes. Preheat oven to 350oF. Place one frank in each roll, spoon equal amounts of sauce mixture over franks. Close roll and wrap securely in foil. Heat for 20 minutes, turning packages after 10 minutes.

CHAPTER FIVE: CHICKEN FOR BARBECUING: America's Love Affair with an Old Flame is Heating Up!

PHOTO: We have four good barbecue photos that might go with this chapter. They're paperclipped in section labeled page 223.

Are you about to barbecue something? Then you're part of an ancient tradition. Barbecuing is actually man's oldest form of cooking; the outdoors was man's first kitchen and an open fire his first stove. The earliest cooking method was to lay food on smoldering embers or impale it on sticks held over a fire or dying coals.

It wasn't until the 1950s, however, that backyard barbecuing as we know it began to catch on. It may surprise you, but auto mogul Henry Ford played a major role in this$and it had nothing to do with his automobiles. Ford's contribution to backyard barbecuing was the invention of the charcoal briquet. In the late 1920s, it was Ford who had the better idea of grinding charcoal, combining it with a starch, and re-forming it into uniform pillow shaped briquets. These charcoal briquets burned more consistently and more evenly than randomly sized and shaped lumps of charcoal.

People immediately began using charcoal briquets for industrial purposes, but backyard grills weren't readily available yet. In the 1950s, when backyard grills became widely available, and outdoor cooking really began to take off. The combination of outdoor grills and the charcoal briquets made barbecuing so easy and reliable, that today, according to a Barbecue Industry Association survey, seven out of ten American households own a barbecue grill, and we use them about 1.5 billion times a year total.

Frank and I also barbecue, but it took some learning on my part. In spite of being someone who loves to cook, before marrying Frank, I'd never barbecued. I'd never even thought to buy an outdoor grill.

What I'd been missing! Frank does own a barbecue, a nice handsome one that can manage chickenburgers for our combined eighteen children and grandchildren all at once. I love it, because we can all be outdoors, playing volley ball or watching the young ones, with their arsenal of squirt guns, as they gang up on Frank$and the beauty of it all is that no one has to miss a moment of the fun by having to go into the kitchen to fuss with dinner.

If you've been barbecuing for years, skip ahead to the recipes. But if you're like me and still new at it, here are some tips that can help you get uniformly good results. The tips come from the Perdue food scientists and home economists, from Cooperative Extension and from the Barbecue Industry Association.

_Start with a clean grill. Removing old ashes assures good air circulation, and cleaning away any cooked- on bits of food results in better flavor and quality.

_Be sure to wash everything after handling raw meat. Don't use the same plate for the cooked meat that you used for the uncooked meat unless you've washed it in between.

_Coat grate with vegetable cooking spray, or brush with cooking oil to prevent food from sticking.

_If the basting sauce contains oil, however, do not grease the grill; too much oil causes flare-ups.

_Prepare the fire a half hour or more before grilling. For quick lighting, use a chimney starter with crumpled newspaper in the bottom and briquets or charcoal above. Or stack the charcoal in a pyramid shape and light with a liquid or electric starter, following the manufacturer's directions. Charcoal is ready for cooking when it's 80% ashy grey in daylight, glowing red at night. This usually takes about 25 to 30 minutes.

_Toss a handful of aromatic wood chips such as mesquite, hickory, alder, or fruitwood chips over the coals. They'll create a whole new dimension of flavor without adding any extra calories.

_Check the temperature of the fire before cooking food to prevent over- or under-cooking. For most of the recipes in this chapter, the fire should be medium-hot with a single, even layer of coals lightly covered with grey ash. It's relatively simple to judge the temperature of a charcoal fire. To do this, hold your hand, palm side down, at cooking height:

HOT - You can hold your hand over the coals for only 2 seconds.

MEDIUM-HOT - You can hold your hand over the coals 3 to 4 seconds.

MEDIUM - You can hold your hand over the coals 4 to 5 seconds.

_Be patient. If the fire hasn't cooled down adequately, do not be tempted to put your chicken on to cook - unless you like "blackened bird" a lot more than I do.

_If you're dieting and want to remove the chicken's skin, do so after cooking, not before. Without some kind of covering, the chicken will dry out and toughen before it finishes cooking.

_Turn chicken frequently, about every 5 minutes to insure even doneness and to prevent blistering.

_If flare-ups occur, remove the food for a few moments and sprinkle water lightly over the flames, or smother them by covering the grill. A friend of mine who works for a volunteer fire department keeps a laundry squirt bottle handy for flare-ups.

_To increase the heat, you can push coals together, add more coals or lower the grilling surface, or fan the fire and tap the ashes from the coals.

_To decrease heat, raise the cooking grid or sprinkle coals with a little water.

_Cook white-meat poultry until juices run clear and the meat reaches an internal temperature of 170o to 175oF and dark meat to 180o to 185oF on a meat thermometer.

_Grill smaller poultry parts and Cornish game hens directly over a single layer of coals on an open grill or hibachi.

_Grill whole birds and larger parts using the indirect method in a covered grill. Place a drip pan beneath the bird; the pan should be slightly larger than the bird. Fill the pan halfway with water, and surround it with a double layer of coals to provide longer, slower, oven-like cooking. Add extra coals to the outer edge of the fire as needed to extend grilling.

_To reduce the chance of overbrowning, apply tomato- based sauces or those containing sugar or other sweeteners only during last 20 to 30 minutes of grilling.

_To make breast quarters grill more quickly and evenly, cut through the wing joint to break it and bring the wing closer to the grill.

_Chicken should be well-done. If you don't want to take the usual time it takes, cook your chicken partially in the microwave and then finish it on the grill.

_The basic guidelines for timing chicken on the grill are:

Parts$Cook dark meat 30 minutes, white meat 15 minutes, basting and turning every five or so minutes.

Halves$First, grill skin side down for 5 minutes, then cook covered, skin side up, 35-40 minutes.

Wings$10 minutes per side.

Whole$(about 3 and 1/2 pounds…About 1 and 1/4 to 1 and 1/2 hours in a covered grill, 1 and 1/2 to 2 hours on rotisserie.

_Use tongs rather than a fork to turn food gently without losing juices.

_If you plan to use marinade as a sauce to be served with chicken during the meal, be sure to cook it before using. You want to avoid the cross-contamination that can come from contact with the uncooked chicken. Temperatures over 140 degrees will destroy any microbes.

BEER-BECUED CHICKEN Serves 2-4 This is one of the National Chicken Cooking Contest winners. It's been adapted slightly, and this version has the reputation of being particularly popular with men. 1 can (12-ounces) beer 1 tablespoon dark molasses 1 tablespoon onion juice 2 tablespoons lemon juice 1/2 cup ketchup 1 teaspoon salt or to taste 1 chicken, cut in half lengthwise In a shallow dish combine beer, molasses, onion juice, lemon juice, ketchup and salt. Add chicken, cover, and marinate 3 hours or longer, refrigerated. Grill chicken 5 to 6 inches above medium-hot coals for 35 to 45 minutes or until cooked through. Turn and baste with marinade every 10 to 15 minutes.

BONELESS BREASTS TANDOORIServes 4 to 6 In many eastern countries, yogurt is a favorite ingredient for marinades used to flavor and tenderize meats. One of the most famous of these recipes is India's Tandoori Chicken, which takes its name from the clay stove called a tandor in which it is cooked. 8 boneless, skinless chicken breast halves 1 cup plain yogurt 1/2 cup butter or margarine 1/4 cup fresh lemon juice 2 large cloves garlic, minced 1 teaspoon cinnamon 1 teaspoon ground cumin 1 teaspoon ground ginger 1 teaspoon turmeric 2 teaspoons ground coriander salt and ground pepper to taste lemon wedges for garnish 1/2 cup melted butter In large bowl combine yogurt, butter, lemon juice and spices. Place chicken breasts in mixture and turn to coat well. Cover and marinate for 3 hours or longer, refrigerated. Remove chicken from marinade and grill 5 to 6 inches above medium-hot coals for 10 minutes Turn and baste 2 to 3 times with marinade. Serve with lemon wedges.

BRANDY-ORANGE BARBECUED CORNISHServes 2-4 When choosing the brandy for this, I'd recommend a California brandy in preference to an imported one. The California ones tend to be lighter and more fruity, which makes them appropriate for this recipe. 2 fresh Cornish hens 1 tablespoon vegetable oil 2 tablespoons fresh lemon juice, divided 1/2 teaspoon ground ginger, divided salt and ground pepper to taste 1/4 cup orange marmalade 1 tablespoon brandy With kitchen string, tie drumsticks together. Rub hens with oil and 1 tablespoon lemon juice; sprinkle with 1/4 teaspoon ginger, salt and pepper. In small bowl, combine marmalade, brandy, remaining lemon juice and ginger; set aside. Place hens on grill breast side up. Grill, covered 5 to 6-inches above medium-hot coals 50 to 60 minutes. After 40 minutes, brush hens with brandy-orange sauce. Cook, basting 3 to 4 times, until juices run clear with no hint of pink when thigh is pierced. CHICK KEBABSServes 6 These chick kebabs go wonderfully with rice. As someone who grows rice commercially, it hurts me to say this, but for this recipe, I recommend a kind of rice I don't grow, the long grain kind that cooks up fluffy with each grain separate. (I grow short or medium grain rice which is always sticky, no matter how you cook it.) 6 boneless, skinless chicken breast halves 1/4 pound small, fresh mushrooms 1 can (7-1/2-ounces) whole white onions 1 green pepper, cut in one-inch squares Marinade: 1/4 cup oil 2 tablespoons vinegar 1 can (8-ounces) crushed pineapple 1 cup ketchup 2 tablespoons soy sauce 1 teaspoon curry powder 3/4 teaspoon minced fresh rosemary or 1/4 teaspoon dried 2 tablespoons brown sugar 1-1/2 teaspoons salt or to taste 2 teaspoons ground pepper 1 tablespoon fresh lemon juice 1 tablespoon cornstarch 1/2 cup water Cut chicken breasts into 1-inch cubes. Alternate chicken on skewers with mushrooms, onions and green pepper, then lay flat in shallow baking dish. Combine marinade ingredients except flour and water. Pour marinade over skewers. Cover and store in refrigerator 3 to 4 hours or overnight. Baste kebabs with marinade and grill 4 to 5 inches above medium-hot coals for 6 to 8 minutes until chicken is lightly browned and cooked through. In a small bowl dissolve cornstarch in water. Place remaining marinade in a small saucepan. Stir in cornstarch and heat, stirring until sauce is slightly thickened. Serve sauce over kebabs and rice.

CHICKEN ALMONDINE

Serves 6-8

You can save money buying the sesame seeds for this recipe in bulk, either from your supermarket or health food store. The one drawback to buying them in bulk is that they have a limited shelf life and at room temperature, they can develop an off-taste due to rancidity. Keep bulk sesame seeds refrigerated or frozen if you won't be using them in a week or so.

8 boneless, skinless chicken breast halves
1-1/2 teaspoons salt or to taste
1/2 teaspoon paprika
6 tablespoons sesame seeds
8 tablespoons butter or margarine, melted
8 tablespoons sliced almonds
8 tablespoons dry vermouth
aluminum foil

Season chicken with salt and paprika; then roll in sesame seeds. Place each chicken piece in center of piece of foil; fold sides up to vertical position to hold liquids. Place 1 tablespoon butter, 1 tablespoon almonds and 1 tablespoon vermouth on each chicken piece. Close foil over chicken and seal well. Place packets on grill 5 to 6 inches above hot coals. Cook about 20 minutes, turning 2 to 3 times until chicken is cooked through.

CHICKEN TARRAGON

Serves 4

To make breast quarters grill more quickly and evenly, remember to cut through the wing joint to break it and bring the wing closer to the grill.

1 chicken, quartered
1/2 cup fresh lime juice
1/4 cup vegetable oil
1/2 cup chopped onion
1/3 cup chopped fresh tarragon or 2 tablespoons dried
salt and ground pepper to taste

Working from the cut side of breast and thigh quarters, carefully use fingers to separate skin from flesh and form a "pocket." In large bowl, combine lime juice and remaining ingredients. Place chicken in marinade and spoon some marinade between skin and flesh. Cover and refrigerate 1 hour or longer. Drain chicken, reserving marinade. Grill chicken, uncovered, 5 to 6-inches above medium-hot coals 35-45 minutes or until cooked through, turning and basting frequently with marinade.

CHUTNEY BURGERS

Serves 4-6

Try this "Yogurt Sauce" along with the Chutney Burgers. In a small bowl combine 1/2 cup yogurt, 2 tablespoons chopped scallions, 2 teaspoons lemon juice, 1/2 teaspoon sugar, 1/4 teaspoon salt and a dash of Cayenne pepper.

1 package fresh ground chicken (about 1 pound) 2 tablespoons chutney 1 tablespoon fresh lemon juice 1/4 cup chopped scallion 1 teaspoon salt 6 individual pita pockets

In a mixing bowl, combine chicken and remaining seasonings. Form into 4 to 6 burgers. Grill on lightly oiled surface, 5 to 6 inches above medium-hot coals, 5 to 6 minutes per side, or until burgers are cooked through. Serve in lightly toasted pita pockets topped with "Yogurt Sauce".

CONFETTI BURGERSServes 4-6 A neat accompaniment for Confetti Burgers is halved Kaiser rolls, brushed with olive oil flavored with garlic. Place on outer edges of grill a few minutes until lightly toasted. 1 package fresh ground chicken (about 1 pound) 1/4 cup oat bran or bread crumbs 1/4 cup finely chopped onion 1/4 cup diced tomato 1/4 cup finely chopped carrot 1/4 cup finely chopped celery 1/4 cup finely chopped green pepper 1 tablespoon Worcestershire sauce 1 tablespoon fresh lemon juice 1 teaspoon salt 1/2 teaspoon dried thyme 1/4 teaspoon ground black pepper 6 Kaiser rolls

In a mixing bowl combine chicken with vegetables and seasonings. Form into 6 burgers. Grill on lightly oiled surface 5 to 6-inches above medium-hot coals for 4 to 6 minutes per side or until burgers are cooked through. Serve on toasted Kaiser rolls.

CHINESE GRILLED DRUMSTICKSServes 2-4 Hoisin sauce is available in Chinese groceries. It's slightly sweet, and thick, somewhat like ketchup. 5 roaster drumsticks salt and ground pepper to taste 1/4 cup hoisin sauce 2 tablespoons dry sherry 2 tablespoons cider vinegar 2 tablespoons honey 1 teaspoon minced fresh ginger 1 clove garlic, minced Season chicken to taste with salt and pepper. In a shallow bowl combine remaining ingredients. Roll drumsticks in sauce, reserving excess. Wrap drumsticks individually in aluminum foil, adding a spoonful of sauce to each package. Grill 6 to 8-inches from hot coals, or bake 1 hour at 375oF, turning once. Unwrap drumsticks and place on grill, or broiling pan. Pour drippings from foil packages and remaining sauce into a small saucepan and heat. Grill or broil drumsticks turning and basting frequently with sauce for 15 minutes or until cooked through. FIRE EATERS' CHICKENServes 4 This recipe gets its name from the rather large quantity of red pepper. If children and other non-fire eaters will be eating this, you will probably want to decrease the amount of red pepper substantially. 4 boneless, skinless chicken breast halves 3 tablespoons fresh lemon juice 2 tablespoons olive oil 2 garlic cloves, minced 1 teaspoon paprika 1/2 to 1 teaspoon crushed red pepper or to taste 1/2 teaspoon salt or to taste Lemon wedges (optional) In shallow dish, combine lemon juice, olive oil, garlic, paprika, pepper and salt. Add chicken to marinade, turning to coat both sides. Cover and refrigerate 1 hour or longer. Drain chicken, reserving marinade. Grill chicken breasts, uncovered, 5 to 6-inches above medium-hot coals 6 to 8 minutes on each side until cooked through, basting occasionally with marinade. To serve, garnish with lemon wedges. GAME HENS PESTOServes 4 Pesto is a sauce made with basil, parsley, garlic, olive oil and Parmesan cheese. If you're looking for a shortcut, you might be able to find ready-made Pesto in your supermarket. 2 fresh Cornish game hens 1/4 cup olive or salad oil 1/4 cup minced fresh basil or 1 tablespoon dried basil 1/4 cup minced fresh parsley 2 tablespoons grated Parmesan cheese 1 small clove garlic, minced 1/2 teaspoon salt or to taste 1 can (8-ounces) minced clams, drained 2 tablespoons dry white wine (optional) Halve hens lengthwise and remove backbones. Place 1 half on each of four 14-inch squares of heavy duty aluminum foil. Turn up edges of foil. In bowl, blend oil, basil, parsley, cheese, garlic and salt. Add clams and wine. Divide among packets, spooning over hens. Bring two opposite sides of foil together and close packets securely using several folds and turning up ends to seal. Cook 4 to 6 inches above hot coals, 30 to 40 minutes, until cooked through, turning packets twice. Packets may also be baked at 400oF for about 30 minutes.

GRILLED BREAST STEAK SALAD Serves 4 If you have leftovers, use them in a sandwich. 1 roaster boneless breast 3 tablespoons butter or margarine, melted 1-1/2 teaspoons Worcestershire sauce 1/4 teaspoon paprika salt and ground pepper to taste 1/4 cup red wine vinegar 2 teaspoons Dijon mustard 3/4 cup olive or vegetable oil 3 tablespoons minced red onion 3 cups spinach leaves, sliced into 1/2" strips 3 cups thinly sliced red cabbage Flatten breast halves slightly between sheets of plastic wrap. Combine butter, Worcestershire sauce, paprika, salt and pepper. Brush sauce liberally over chicken. Grill 5 to 6 inches above medium-hot coals for 8 to 10 minutes on each side or until cooked through. Remove and slice thinly on the diagonal. Combine vinegar and mustard in a small bowl. Slowly whisk in oil. Add red onion and season with salt and pepper. Place 2 cups spinach and 2 cups cabbage in a salad bowl. Arrange half of the chicken slices over top and spoon half of the dressing over all.

GRILLED CORNISH WITH VEGETABLES Serves 2 If you want to skip tying the legs together, as called for in this recipe, the hens won't hold their shape as well and will look more relaxed. The advantage is that you may feel more relaxed. 2 fresh Cornish game hens salt and ground pepper to taste 2 tablespoons butter or margarine 1 medium carrot, cut into thin strips 1 small leek, cut into thin strips 1 rib celery, cut into thin strips 1/4 cup apple juice 1 tablespoon minced fresh parsley Season hens inside and out with salt and pepper. Tie legs together and fold wings back. Place each hen on an 18-inch square of heavy duty aluminum foil. Dot with butter. Divide vegetables and apple juice among foil pieces. Fold edges up and seal tightly. Place packets on grill 5 to 6 inches above hot coals. Cook 60 to 70 minutes, turning 2 to 3 times until hens are cooked through. Or bake at 400ºF one hour or until juices run clear with no hint of pink when thigh is pierced. Open foil packages carefully and sprinkle with parsley.

GRILLED DRUMSTICKS WITH FRUIT MUSTARD

Serves 2-4

Do you remember in the early 1980s a fast food chain had a popular advertising campaign based on the slogan, "Where's the beef?" One of my favorite Perdue ads is a full page ad showing Frank holding a drumstick with a big bite missing. He's looking out at you, his eyebrows raised quizzically as he asks, "Who cares where the beef is?" This recipe could have been used to cook the drumstick shown in the ad.

5 roaster drumsticks
salt and ground pepper to taste
8 ripe apricots, or 1 can (16-ounces) drained and coarsely chopped
1 tablespoon fresh lemon juice
1/4 cup Dijon mustard
3 tablespoons dark brown sugar
1/4 cup brandy
1 teaspoon Worcestershire sauce

Season drumsticks with salt and pepper. Toss apricots with lemon; add remaining ingredients and toss. Wrap drumsticks individually with aluminum foil, adding a spoonful of sauce to each package. Grill 5 to 6 inches above hot coals or bake at 375ºF for 1 hour, turning once. Unwrap drumsticks and place on grill, or broiling pan. Add drippings from foil packages to remaining sauce. Grill or broil drumsticks turning and basting frequently with sauce for 15 minutes or until cooked through.

GRILLED CUTLETS COSTA DEL SOL

Serves 4

This is one of Perdue's most popular and most requested recipes.

4 roaster boneless thigh cutlets
1/3 cup dry sherry
1 teaspoon paprika
1 teaspoon ground cumin
1 teaspoon sugar
1 teaspoon white vinegar
salt and ground pepper to taste
1 clove garlic, minced

Place cutlets between sheets of plastic wrap and pound to 1/2" thickness. In a shallow dish combine remaining ingredients. Add chicken and marinate for 1 hour or longer, refrigerated. Grill chicken 5 to 6 inches above medium-hot coals for 15 to 20 minutes or until cooked through. Turn and baste with glaze 2 to 3 times.

GRILLED CUTLETS GREEK STYLE WITH OLIVE OIL

Serves 4

Olive growers like to point out that the lowest mortality rates due to cardiovascular disease are found on the Greek island of Crete where olive oil consumption is highest. 4 roaster boneless thigh cutlets 2 cloves garlic, minced 2 tablespoons fresh lemon juice, divided 6 tablespoons olive oil, divided 1/3 cup plain yogurt 1 teaspoon dried oregano salt and ground pepper to taste 4 ripe tomatoes, cut into wedges (3 cups) 2 cucumbers, peeled, halved and cut into 1/2" slices (3/4 cup) 2 tablespoons minced, fresh parsley or mint 1/2 cup pitted ripe olives Place cutlets between two sheets of plastic wrap and pound to 1/4" thickness. In a shallow dish whisk together garlic, 1 tablespoon lemon juice, 2 tablespoons olive oil, yogurt, oregano, salt and pepper. Add cutlets and turn to coat with marinade. Cover and marinate for 3 hours or longer, refrigerated. Grill cutlets 4 to 6 inches above medium-hot coals for 3 to 4 minutes on each side or until cooked through. In a large bowl, combine tomatoes, cucumbers, red onion, black olives, remaining lemon juice, 4 tablespoons olive oil and salt and pepper to taste. Sprinkle with parsley or mint before serving. Cutlets may be served hot with salad as a side dish or served cold sliced and added to salad.

GYPSY BURGERS Serves 4-6 What I like best about chicken burgers, as opposed to hamburgers, is that chicken burgers don't shrink much when you cook them. 1 package fresh ground chicken 3/4 cup chopped scallion, divided 1/2 cup sour cream, divided 2 teaspoons paprika 1 teaspoon salt 1/4 teaspoon ground pepper Pinch Cayenne pepper 8 to 12 slices Italian or French bread

In a mixing bowl, combine chicken, 1/3 cup scallions, 2 tablespoons sour cream, and remaining ingredients. Form into 4 to 6 burgers. Grill on lightly oiled surface 5 to 6 inches above medium-hot coals, 5 to 6 minutes per side or until cooked through. Serve on toasted slices of Italian or French bread, topped with sour cream and scallions. PHOTO: Hawaiian glazed wings HAWAIIAN GLAZED WINGSServes 2-4 The natural juiciness of chicken wings makes them a good choice for barbecuing. This can make either a nice meal for a few, or appetizers for several. 10 chicken wings 1/2 cup vegetable oil 2 tablespoons fresh lemon juice 1/2 teaspoon seasoned salt or to taste Marmalade Pineapple Glaze: 1/4 cup orange marmalade 1/4 cup pineapple preserves 1/2 cup soy sauce 1 teaspoon Dijon mustard 2 tablespoons white wine vinegar In a large bowl toss wings with vegetable oil, lemon juice and seasoned salt. In a small bowl combine glaze ingredients. Drain wings and grill 6 to 8 inches above medium-hot coals for about 20 minutes or until golden brown and cooked through. Turn and baste 2 to 3 times with glaze. HERB BARBECUED BREASTSServes 4 Frank always removes the skin from chicken, and often, that means losing some of the herbs and spices. I like this recipe because even if you remove the skin at the end of the barbecuing, the flavoring is still there. 4 chicken breast halves 1/2 cup softened butter or margarine 2 tablespoons chopped scallions 2 tablespoons minced, fresh parsley 1 and 1/2 teaspoons minced, fresh rosemary, or 1/2 teaspoon dried 1/2 teaspoon salt or to taste 1 small clove garlic, minced 1/8 teaspoon ground pepper Working from the wide "neck end" of breasts use finger tips to carefully separate skin from meat to form a pocket. In a small saucepan combine remaining ingredients. Place about 2 tablespoons of butter mixture in pocket of each breast. Close skin flap at neck edge with a small skewer or toothpick. Melt remaining butter mixture and reserve for basting. Grill chicken 6 to 8 inches above medium-hot coals for 25 to 30 minutes or until cooked through turning and basting chicken every 8 to 10 minutes with butter.

HONEY MUSTARD GRILLED HENS Serves 2 I've found that hens cook a little faster and are more attractive when served if you remove the backbone before cooking. 2 fresh Cornish game hens salt and ground pepper to taste 4 tablespoons butter or margarine 2 tablespoons honey 1 1/2 tablespoons Dijon mustard 1 tablespoon Worcestershire sauce Halve hens and remove backbones. (See page ___ for directions on doing this.) Season with salt and pepper. In a small saucepan, melt butter; stir in remaining ingredients. Grill hens 6 to 8 inches above hot coals 20 to 30 minutes or until cooked through, turning often. Baste with sauce during last 10 minutes of cooking time.

HOT AND SPICY PICK-OF-THE-CHICK Serves 4-6 Are you familiar with the spice, "cumin", called for in this recipe? It's the dried fruit or seed of a plant in the parsley family. It's sometimes substituted for caraway seed and is a principal ingredient in both curry powder and chili powder. 1 jar (5-ounces) roasted peppers, drained 1 can (4-ounces) mild green chilies, drained 2 tablespoons brown sugar 2 tablespoons vegetable oil 2 tablespoons lime juice 1-1/2 teaspoons Tabasco 1 teaspoon ground cumin 1 teaspoon salt or to taste 2 to 3 sprigs fresh coriander (optional) 1 package chicken parts (about 3 pounds) In food processor or blender, combine all ingredients except chicken; puree until smooth. Set aside 1/2 cup sauce. Grill chicken, uncovered, 5 to 6-inches above medium-hot coals 40 to 50 minutes or until cooked through, turning and basting with remaining sauce 3 to 4 times during grilling. Serve reserved 1/2 cup sauce as a condiment with grilled chicken. Oriental Grill "KUNG FU" CUTLETS Serves 4 When you see the sweet potatoes called for in this recipe, you might wonder, "Is there's a difference between sweet potatoes and yams?" And if there is a difference, "Does it matter?" According to sweet potato grower Tom Archibald from California, there is and it does. "The sweet potato's texture is close to an Irish potato's, while the yam's is moister and less firm and doesn't hold up as well," he says. "You can tell the difference between them because the sweet potato is light-skinned, while the yam has a bronze-colored or reddish skin." 4 boneless, skinless chicken breast halves or 1 package thin sliced roaster breast 2 sweet potatoes, scrubbed but not peeled 8 scallions, trimmed 1 tablespoon soy sauce 1 teaspoon sesame or vegetable oil 1/2 teaspoon ground pepper 1/2 cup tonkatsu sauce (recipe follows, or use bottled version) Place chicken breasts between sheets of plastic wrap and pound to 1/2 inch thickness. Skip previous step if using thin sliced roaster breast. Cut sweet potatoes into 1/2- inch slices. Place chicken and potatoes in a shallow bowl with scallions, soy sauce, oil and pepper; toss well. Grill cutlets and potato slices 6 to 8 inches above medium- hot coals for 8 to 10 minutes per side or until cutlets are cooked through and potato slices tender. Grill scallions 10 minutes, turning once. Serve grilled cutlets and vegetables with tonkatsu sauce as condiment; add a favorite cole slaw as side dish. Tonkatsu Sauce: In small bowl, combine 1/4 cup sweet and sour sauce, 1 tablespoon soy sauce, 2 teaspoon white vinegar, and 1 teaspoon Worcestershire sauce. LEMON SPECIAL CHICKEN Serves 2-4 If you don't want to barbecue a half chicken, substitute chicken parts. See table on page 12 for amounts to equal a whole chicken. 1 chicken, cut in half lengthwise 4 tablespoons butter or margarine, melted 1/2 teaspoon paprika 2 tablespoons sugar 2 tablespoons fresh lemon juice 1 teaspoon Worcestershire sauce 1 teaspoon salt or to taste 1/2 teaspoon ground pepper Grill chicken halves 5 to 6 inches above medium-hot coals for 35 to 45 minutes or until cooked through. In a small saucepan combine remaining ingredients. Make sauce of butter or margarine, paprika, sugar, lemon juice and Worcestershire. Turn and baste chicken with butter sauce 2 to 3 times. MAHOGANY BARBECUED HENSServes 2 People often ask Frank if a Cornish game hen is a separate breed from regular chickens. The answer is mostly no and a little bit yes. Cornish game hens are young chickens, usually around five weeks; if they were just a couple of weeks older, they'd be sold for broilers, except for the Perdue ones. Perdue Cornish come from the Roaster breed which Perdue geneticist Norman Lupean developed, and which is only available through Perdue. Unlike broilers, roasters reach market size at twelve weeks. Both Perdue Cornish and the Oven Stuffer Roasters were bred to have the broadest, meatiest breasts in the industry. 2 fresh Cornish game hens 1/4 cup mustard 1/4 cup grape jelly 2 tablespoons oil Halve hens and remove backbones. In a small bowl combine remaining ingredients. Grill 5 to 6 inches above medium-hot coals for 30 to 40 minutes until cooked through, turning 2 to 3 times. Baste with mustard mixture during last 15 minutes.

MEXICALI CHICKEN

Serves 4-6

When you buy a chili powder for use in a Mexican dish like this one, you can be pretty sure that as long as you stick with the same brand, it will be about the same "heat" next year as it was last year. Having this kind of quality control is difficult because, first, there are more than 5000 known varieties of chilies, each with their own degree of "heat" and second, the same variety grown in a different climate or different year will vary considerably. The chili powder manufacturers get a consistent product by adjusting the formulations each year.

1/3 cup fresh lime juice
1/3 cup white vinegar
1 teaspoon chili powder
1 teaspoon salt or to taste
1/4 teaspoon ground pepper
1 whole roaster breast
2 tablespoons chopped, mild green chilies
1/4 cup ketchup
Tabasco

In large bowl, combine lime juice, vinegar, cumin, chili powder, salt and pepper. Place breast in marinade; cover and refrigerate 1 hour or longer. When coals are hot, arrange around drip pan filled halfway with water, close all vents. Drain breast, reserving marinade. Place breast skin side down on grill over drip pan. Grill, covered, 50 to 55 minutes, turning occasionally. Meanwhile, in small saucepan over medium-high heat, combine reserved marinade, green chilies, ketchup and Tabasco to taste; bring to a boil. Reduce heat to low; simmer until slightly thickened. Remove from heat and brush over chicken during last 10 minutes of cooking time. Serve chicken with remaining sauce.

Grilled Fiesta Lunch

MEXICALI CUTLETS

Serves 4

You could just heat the cutlets in the microwave, but the smoke from the barbecue will produce a particularly delicious result.

1 package breaded chicken breast cutlets, ready to eat
4 slices Monterey Jack or mild cheddar cheese
8 flour tortillas
1 ripe tomato, sliced
1 ripe avocado, sliced
1/2 cup sour cream
1/4 cup Mexican salsa

Grill cutlets 5 to 6-inches above hot coals 3 to 4 minutes on each side or until crisp, browned and sizzling. In last 3 to 4 minutes, place a slice of cheese on each cutlet to melt. While cutlets are grilling, sprinkle tortillas with few drops of water and wrap in aluminum foil. Warm tortillas along edge of grill. To serve, remove grilled cutlets to serving plates and top with tomato and avocado slices; add dollops of sour cream and salsa. Pass warm tortillas.

MISSISSIPPI SMOKY BARBECUED DRUMSTICKS

Serves 2

Try serving these with drumsticks frills for a special decorative touch. Fold heavy white paper (7-inches by 9- inches) in half, lengthwise. Fold in half lengthwise again and tape long edges closed. This produces a strip measuring 9-inches by 1-3/4-inches. Cut strip into two 4- 1/2-inch strips. On each, slash 1-inch cuts at 1/4-inch intervals along the entire length of the untaped folded edge. To "fluff" frills, press top of slashed edge. Tape frills in place around drumsticks just before serving.

5 roaster drumsticks
salt and ground pepper to taste
1/4 cup finely chopped onion
1/4 cup finely chopped green pepper
1/2 cup ketchup
1 tablespoon Worcestershire sauce
1-1/2 teaspoons liquid smoke (optional)
2 tablespoons dark brown sugar
2 tablespoons cider vinegar
1/2 teaspoon cinnamon
8 to 12 drops Tabasco, or to taste

Season drumsticks with salt and pepper. In a shallow dish combine remaining ingredients. Roll drumsticks in sauce, reserving excess. Wrap drumsticks individually in aluminum foil, adding a spoonful of sauce to each package. Grill 6 to 8-inches from hot coals, or bake at 375oF 1 hour, turning once. Unwrap drumsticks and place on grill, or broiling pan. Add drippings from foil packages to remaining sauce. Grill or broil drumsticks turning and basting frequently with sauce for 15 minutes or until cooked through.

NORTH CAROLINA GRILLED CHICKEN

Serves 4-6

This was a National Chicken Cooking Contest winner.

2 chickens, cut in half lengthwise
1 cup butter or margarine (2 sticks), melted
2 envelopes (6-ounces each) Italian salad dressing mix
1/2 cup fresh lime juice
1 teaspoon salt or to taste

Place chicken in a shallow dish. In a measuring cup combine remaining ingredients and pour over chicken; cover and refrigerate. Melt butter or margarine in saucepan. Marinate turning occasionally, for 3 to 4 hours or overnight. Grill chicken 5 to 6 inches above medium-hot coals for

35 to 45 minutes or until cooked through. Turn and baste with marinade every 10 to 15 minutes.

PEPPERY GRILLED THIGH SALAD
Serves 4

The arugula called for in this recipe is not essential and you can substitute watercress or even iceberg lettuce if you have to. But if you can find it, it's a fresh attractive taste. I used to grow arugula in my back yard garden, using seeds a friend brought back for me from Italy.

4 boneless roaster thigh cutlets
1 teaspoon coarsely ground or cracked black pepper
3 tablespoons Worcestershire sauce, divided
1/2 cup olive oil or vegetable oil, divided
salt to taste
1 tablespoon Dijon mustard
2 tablespoons wine vinegar
1 tablespoon minced shallot or scallion
1 small head bibb or Boston lettuce, torn into pieces
1 bunch arugula, well rinsed, torn into pieces
1 head Belgian endive, torn into pieces
1/2 pound green beans, cooked tender-crisp
1 tablespoon minced fresh basil (optional)
1 tablespoon minced fresh parsley

Open cutlets and flatten slightly to even thickness; press pepper into both sides of cutlets and place in a shallow baking dish. Add 2 tablespoons Worcestershire sauce; turn chicken to coat well. Cover and refrigerate 1 hour or longer. Remove cutlets from marinade; brush with 1 tablespoon oil and sprinkle lightly with salt. Grill cutlets, uncovered, 5 to 6-inches above medium-hot coals 25 to 35 minutes or until chicken is cooked through, turning occasionally. In salad bowl, combine mustard, vinegar and shallot. Gradually whisk in remaining oil. Slice warm cutlets and add any meat juices to dressing. Arrange greens around edges of 4 dinner plates. Toss chicken and beans with dressing and mound equal portions in middle of greens. To serve, drizzle salads with any remaining dressing and sprinkle with minced herbs.

PRAIRIE BARBECUED CHICKEN
Serves 2-4

Besides adding flavor, vinegar makes an excellent tenderizing agent in this$or any$marinade.

1/2 cup butter or margarine, melted
1/2 cup cider vinegar
1 bottle (15-ounces) ketchup
1 teaspoon salt or to taste
1 teaspoon ground pepper
1 cup water
1 chicken, cut in half lengthwise

In a shallow dish combine butter, vinegar, ketchup, salt, pepper and water. Add chicken and turn to coat well; cover and refrigerate. Marinate chicken several hours or overnight. Grill 5 to 6 inches above medium-hot coals for 35 to 45 minutes or until cooked through. Baste with marinade and turn 3 to 4 times.

PHOTO: "Spring "B" list, 1985, Father's Day Barbecue PROVENCAL HERB DRUMSTICKSServes 2-3 The flavorful combination called "herbes de Provence", consisting of basil, thyme, oregano, and other herbs, is typically used in marinades in the south of France, where grilling is often done over cuttings from grape vines. 6 chicken drumsticks 1/2 cup red wine 1/3 cup water 1 tablespoon wine vinegar 2 garlic cloves, minced 1 1/2 teaspoons minced fresh basil or 1/2 teaspoon dried 1-1/2 teaspoons minced fresh thyme or 1/2 teaspoon dried 1-1/2 teaspoons minced fresh oregano or 1/2 teaspoon dried 1 bay leaf 1 tablespoon tomato paste 2 teaspoons anchovy paste (optional) 1/2 teaspoon salt or to taste 1/4 teaspoon ground pepper 1 tablespoon olive oil With fork, pierce drumsticks to help seasonings to penetrate. In large bowl, combine remaining ingredients except oil; whisk in oil. Add chicken to marinade; cover and refrigerate 1 hour or longer. Grill drumsticks, uncovered, 5 to 6-inches above medium-hot coals 35 to 45 minutes or until cooked through, turning and basting frequently with marinade. RUSSIAN GRILLED CORNISHServes 2-3 For a traditional Russian Cornish, use a heavy iron skillet to weight hens while grilling. Called tabaka-style in Russia, pressed chicken is popular because it browns quickly and holds its shape well. 2 fresh Cornish game hens 6 tablespoons fresh lemon juice 1 clove garlic, minced 1 tablespoon vegetable oil Kosher salt and pepper to taste lemon wedges (optional) With poultry shears or sharp knife, cut along both sides of backbone and remove. On flat surface, spread out hens skin side up and press down on breast bones to flatten. In a dish combine lemon juice and garlic. Add hens to marinade, turning to coat well. Cover and refrigerate 1 hour or longer. Remove hens from marinade, rub lightly with oil and sprinkle with salt and pepper. Place hens on grill, skin side up, and top with a heavy iron skillet or other pan filled with 1 pound heat-proof object, to flatten. Grill, 5 to 6 inches above medium-hot coals. After 15 minutes turn hens and replace weight. Continue grilling for another 15 to 20 minutes or until hens are well browned and cooked through. To serve, garnish hens with lemon wedges.

SANTA FE CHICKEN HERO

Serves 4-5

Thin-sliced roaster breast couldn't be easier or faster to grill for this hearty update of the submarine/hoagy/hero sandwich. This is a complete Tex-Mex meal in one.

1 roaster thin-sliced boneless breast (1 1/4 pounds) or 4 skinless, boneless, chicken breast halves butterflied
1 tablespoon vegetable oil
Salt and ground pepper to taste
Cayenne
Chili powder
5 to 6 thin slices Monterey Jack cheese with chilies
5 to 6 slices French or Italian bread
2 tablespoons melted butter or margarine
5 to 6 leaves Romaine lettuce
1 tomato, thinly sliced
1 avocado, peeled, pitted, sliced and tossed with lemon juice
1/2 cup prepared salsa

Rub chicken lightly with oil and season with salt, pepper, Cayenne and chili powder. Grill, 5 to 6-inches above medium-hot coals about 2 minutes on each side. Top chicken with slices of cheese; grill 1 to 2 minutes longer or until cheese is melted. Brush bread with melted butter; grill alongside chicken 1 to 2 minutes on each side until golden brown. To serve, place a lettuce leaf on each toasted bread slice. Evenly divide chicken, slices of tomato and avocado on top. Serve sandwiches open-faced with salsa.

SEASONED BARBECUED CHICKEN

Serves 2-4

This recipe calls for Sauterne wine, which is a fairly sweet wine. You can use another white wine if you can't find Sauterne; the results will still be good, just different.

1 chicken, cut in half lengthwise
1 cup Sauterne wine
1/2 cup oil
1/2 cup fresh lemon juice
1/4 cup soy sauce
1 tablespoon onion juice
1 clove garlic, minced
1/2 teaspoon salt
1/2 teaspoon ground pepper

Place chicken in a shallow dish and add remaining ingredients. Turn chicken to coat with marinade. Cover and refrigerate for 3 hours or longer. Grill chicken 5 to 6

CHAPTER SIX CHICKEN FOR CROWDS

Do you have a wedding coming up? A school reunion? Or you just want to have the crowd over? Well guess what! I recommend chicken for the menu! Seriously, it's a good choice because it's on almost everyone's diet, most people like it, and it's probably the most economical main course that can be served to crowds.

Frank and I both enjoy entertaining. There are many months in the year when we entertain 50 associates (that's the term used at Perdue Farms for employees) each week, and at Christmas time, it has gotten up to 300 in a week.

People who know that Frank and I entertain a lot sometimes ask why I don't have the parties catered. The fact is, I don't want to hire somebody to do what I enjoy doing anyway.

Besides, it wouldn't fit in with our lifestyle to have catered affairs. Frank is actually a frugal and down-to- earth man. He travels economy class, is careful to turn the lights off when we leave the house, and before we married, he cooked for himself and washed his own dishes. (Now I do it.)

It's a real compliment when Frank says that someone is "tight as the bark on an oak tree."

Still, I know we're all busy, so I'm in favor of any shortcuts that help save time even if they cost a little extra. And yet, as a former New England Yankee, I am always in favor of spending money carefully. Here are some of the tips that I've learned that may help you, whether you're cooking for eight or a hundred:

_Plan a simple menu with everything done in advance, except simple heating or reheating. Most cookbooks suggest that you have only a few dishes that require last minute work, but I don't want the hassle of worrying about any; I've found that last minute things always come up, and it's wonderful to know that they're not going to upset your schedule or leave you in a state of frazzlement. In my own case, I'm always working harder the day before the party than the day of the party.

_Check that you've got refrigerator or freezer space for all perishables.

_Check that you have the pots and pans and storage containers for the foods you'll be preparing.

_Write a detailed schedule for yourself including the menu and shopping list. I like to have a copy of the menu visible on my refrigerator, partly because it gives me confidence as I check off each dish as it's completed, but mostly because I remember one party when I forgot a dish that I had cooked and was faced with leftover string beans for thirty.

_This tip has nothing to do with poultry, but it's worked so well for me I'll share it anyway. When the occasion is special enough so that you're using a florist, (a wedding? an anniversary?) your flower budget will go further if you'll call the florist a week ahead and tell him or her your color scheme and what you're willing to spend. The florist will know which flowers are in over supply and therefore a bargain, and given a week, he or she will have the time to place an order with the wholesaler for the ones which are a good buy. You won't necessarily spend less, but you're likely to get considerably more for your money.

_Keep food safety in mind as you work. Keep perishable food, such as chicken, in the refrigerator except when you're working with it. Prepare food in batches and have out only what you're using. When refrigerating foods, have them in small enough batches so that they'll cool quickly.

_If you're serving wine, make it white wine rather than red wine. I say that not because white wine is supposed to go with chicken (some of the more robust recipes for chicken go beautifully with red wine), but because white wine is less of a menace to your carpets.

_If it's a buffet and people will be balancing plates on their laps, serve foods that are already bite-sized and that don't require cutting with a knife and fork.

_Just because you're not having it catered doesn't mean you have to do it all yourself. If you're near a college campus, see if the food service people at the student cafeteria would be willing to make the vegetables or other side dishes. Also, check the cafeteria at a local factory or processing plant. Sometimes these people will moonlight and make large batches of your favorite recipe for you. They've got the equipment, and in my experience, they're pleased to have the extra income. Also, they're frequently less expensive than restaurants and they're apt to be much, much less expensive than a caterer.

_A crowd seldom consumes more than 3-ounces of cooked protein total, per person, and that includes whatever protein is part of the appetizers as well as the main course. However, I usually have closer to 4-ounces per person available, just for "sociable security." If you plan on just under 4-ounces each, you'll almost certainly have leftovers, but at least you won't run out. Another way of calculating is that a breast and a wing per person will insure that you'll have more than enough. (Adjust this depending on whether you're entertaining toddlers or professional football players or$the biggest eaters$older teenage boys.) Also, keep in mind how much else you're serving. At our parties, I've seen that I'll always have some leftovers if I allow a half cup serving per person for each of the following: starches, vegetables, and salad, plus a serving and a quarter of bread. That's assuming that there have been a couple of small appetizers before, and that the main course will be followed by dessert.

_When you're multiplying recipes, keep in mind that cooking times may be different if you change the recipe size. A larger amount of food may take longer to cook; a smaller amount may be overcooked in the same time. ILLUSTRATION: ORIENTAL MINI DRUMSTICKS FROM CHICKEN WINGS CURRIED CHICKEN FROM BONELESS BREAST SANTA FE CHICKEN OR BONELESS THIGHS PHOTO OF ALL THREE IN FILES PHOTO: Chicken "nibbles" just right for... - 6 DIPS AND SPREADS - 5 CHICKEN "NIBBLES" TAKE THE HEAT OUT OF SUMMER ENTERTAINING Summer parties come in all shapes and sizes. Some are small and happen on the spur of the moment. Others are great boisterous affairs that roll across the lawn or down the beach. They're fun. They're happy. They also can be lots of work, but one of the nicest shortcuts I know is the pre-cooked nuggets, tenders, or wings. Straight from the package or warmed for serving, they're extra tasty dunked into a quick dip. I sometimes have an assortment of store- bought mustards available, each in a pretty dish. Or, when there's more time, I'd use one of these Perdue recipes for dips. COOL AND CREAMY AVOCADO DIPMakes about 1-1/

Home economist Pat Cobe developed many of the dips for Perdue. I asked her how she got her ideas, and learned that when composing a recipe she starts out by imagining all the dips she's sampled at restaurants or food conventions or parties, or ones she's read about in magazines and cookbooks. Then in her imagination, she puts together the best ideas from all of them. As she sorts these ideas around in her mind, she'll come up with something new, and then she'll test it. Of all the ones she thinks of, the only ones that she would consider actually recommending to Perdue, would have to meet her criteria of being "real food for real people." Like this one. 4 cups 1 ripe avocado, peeled and seed removed 1/4 cup chopped scallions 1 tablespoon lime or lemon juice 1/2 teaspoon salt or to taste 1/2 cup sour cream In small bowl with fork, mash avocado. Add green scallions, lime juice and salt; blend well. Stir in sour cream. Serve immediately or refrigerate until ready to serve. CREOLE DIPMakes about 1 cup 2/3 cup bottled chili sauce 1 tablespoon prepared horseradish (optional) 1 tablespoon Worcestershire sauce 1 tablespoon minced fresh parsley 1 tablespoon minced scallion 1 tablespoon minced celery In small bowl, combine all ingredients. If time allows, let stand at room temperature 1 hour for flavors to blend. GARLICKY SWEET-SOUR DIPMakes 3/4 cup 2/3 cup packed brown sugar 1/3 cup chicken broth 1 tablespoon soy sauce 1 clove garlic, minced 2 tablespoons cider vinegar 1 tablespoon cornstarch In small saucepan, combine brown sugar, broth, soy sauce and garlic; mix well. In cup, blend vinegar and cornstarch until smooth; stir into saucepan and place over medium heat. Bring to a boil; cook 3 to 5 minutes until mixture thickens and becomes slightly reduced, stirring frequently. Serve warm or at room temperature. MEXICALI CHEESE DIPMakes about 2 cups 1 can (11-ounces) condensed Cheddar cheese soup 1 cup shredded Monterey Jack cheese with Jalapeno peppers 1/2 teaspoon ground cumin 1/2 cup sour cream 1/4 cup chopped pimentos or tomatoes Tabasco (optional) In small saucepan, combine undiluted soup, shredded cheese and cumin. Place over low heat and cook until cheese is completely melted, stirring constantly. Remove from heat; stir in sour cream, pimentos and hot pepper sauce to taste, if desired. To serve, keep warm in fondue pot, chafing dish or heatproof bowl set on warming tray. RED PEPPER DIPMakes about 1-1/3 cups 1 jar (7-ounces) roasted red peppers, drained 1 clove garlic, quartered 1/2 teaspoon ground cumin 1 cup plain lowfat yogurt In blender or food processor, puree red peppers, garlic and cumin. Add yogurt; blend or process a few seconds just until mixed. Chill several hours or overnight to blend flavors. SPICY CRANBERRY - ORANGE DIPMakes about 1 cup 1 cup prepared cranberry sauce 2 tablespoons fresh orange juice 1 tablespoon port or Marsala wine (optional) 1 tablespoon fresh lemon juice 3/4 teaspoon dry mustard 1/2 teaspoon ground ginger In blender or food processor, puree all ingredients. If time allows, let stand at room temperature 1 hour for flavors to blend. APPETIZERS - 14 CHICKEN COCKTAIL PUFFS Makes 36 puffs The cocktail puff is great when stuffed with chicken. I sometimes keep these puffs, unfilled, in the freezer to have available when I need something on short notice. You don't need to thaw them before stuffing. Cocktail Puffs 1/4 cup water 3 tablespoons butter or margarine 1/8 teaspoon salt 1/4 cup flour 1 egg, unbeaten 1/4 cup grated Swiss cheese Preheat oven to 350oF. In a saucepan over medium heat, heat butter in water until melted. Add salt and flour all at once and stir vigorously until ball forms in center of pan. Remove from heat and let stand 5 minutes. Add egg and beat until smooth, add cheese. Mixture should be very stiff. Drop by teaspoonful on baking sheet and bake for about 40 minutes or until surface is free from beads of moisture. Turn off oven and prop door open slightly by putting a pot holder in the crack. Allow puffs to cool in oven. Slice crosswise for stuffing. Filling 2 cups cooked chicken, minced 1/4 cup minced celery 3 tablespoons minced canned pimento 2 tablespoons fresh lemon juice 1 tablespoon finely chopped onion 1 tablespoon minced fresh tarragon or basil 1/4 cup mayonnaise or salad dressing 1/2 teaspoon salt or to taste 1/8 teaspoon ground pepper In a mixing bowl combine chicken, celery, pimento, lemon juice, onion and tarragon lightly with mayonnaise. Season with salt and pepper. Fill each puff with about 2 teaspoons of filling.

CHICKEN FRANK CARAWAY & KRAUT ROLL-UPS

Makes about 64 You can reheat the "Roll-Ups" by toasting briefly under the broiler after slicing. 2 tubes (10-ounces each) refrigerated white dinner loaf 2 tablespoons German-style mustard 1 can (7-ounces) sauerkraut, drained 1 egg, beaten, for glaze 8 chicken franks 4 tablespoons caraway seeds Preheat oven to 350F. Meanwhile, gently unroll loaf into a 12-inch square, pinching slashed portions together to seal. With sharp knife, cut dough into quarters. Spread each piece of dough with mustard and a thin layer of sauerkraut to within 1/2 inch of edge. Brush edge lightly with egg. Place a frank on left side of 1 piece of dough and roll up tightly. Place roll, seam side down, on a greased baking sheet. Repeat with remaining franks and dough. Brush rolls with egg and sprinkle with caraway seeds. Bake for 15 minutes until golden brown. Remove rolls to a cutting board and allow to cool several minutes. With serrated knife, slice each roll into 8 small "roll-ups." Serve immediately.

CHICKEN LIVER LOVERLIES

Makes 50 puffs It's not quite a cookie. It's not quite a puff. It's not quite a fritter. It's just something very special. 12 chicken livers (about 1 lb.) 3/4 cup butter or margarine, divided 1 cup water 1 cup flour 4 eggs, unbeaten 1 envelope (1-3/8 oz.) dehydrated onion soup mix. In a large skillet over medium heat, melt 1/4 cup butter. Add chicken livers and saute for 6 to 8 minutes; chop finely. In a saucepan over medium heat, melt remaining butter with water. Add flour all at once and stir vigorously until ball forms in center of pan. Add eggs, one at a time, beating after each egg. Stir in livers and soup mix. Preheat oven to 375oF. Drop by teaspoonful on baking sheet and bake for 25 to 30 minutes until puffed and golden brown.

CHICKEN LIVER PATE

Makes 12 I like this on rye crackers. 12 chicken livers (about 1 lb.) 1/2 cup butter or margarine 1 medium onion, finely chopped 4 eggs, hard cooked 1/2 teaspoon Tabasco In a large skillet over medium heat, melt butter. Add livers and onions and saute for 8 to 10 minutes. Put all ingredients in blender or food processor and blend until smooth. CHICKEN PARTY SANDWICH FILLINGMakes approximately 50 Try using different shaped cookie cutters or use different colors of bread. It's nice on open sandwiches—garnished with an olive slice or a lemon sliver. 1 cup cooked, ground chicken 1/2 teaspoon salt or to taste 1/4 cup mayonnaise or salad dressing 2 tablespoons fresh lemon juice 2 tablespoons milk 1 teaspoon sugar In a bowl combine all ingredients. Spread on bread or salted crackers. CHICKEN QUICHE Makes 32 narrow wedges For an attractive and professional presentation, make miniature quiches by lining the inside bottom of your muffin pans with pie dough, forming little tart shells. Then add the filling. I see a lot of these at Washington parties. 1 tablespoon butter or margarine, softened 2 pie shells (approximately 9") 1 cup cooked chicken cut in small pieces 1 cup grated Swiss cheese 12 slices crisp, cooked bacon, crumbled 4 eggs, slightly beaten 2 cups heavy cream 1/2 teaspoon salt or to taste 1/8 teaspoon nutmeg 1/8 teaspoon sugar 1/8 teaspoon Cayenne pepper 1/8 teaspoon ground pepper Preheat oven to 425oF. Rub butter or margarine on pie shells. Put chicken, grated cheese and bacon in pie shells. In a mixing bowl combine all remaining ingredients and pour into shells. Bake for 15 minutes. Reduce heat to 300oF and bake 40 minutes longer. Cut in narrow pie wedges for serving. PHOTO: A storybook reception - garden dining on Chicken... - 6

CURRIED CHICKEN AND FRUIT KEBABS WITH YOGURT SAUCE Makes 25-30

Be sure to look at the accompanying illustration. This looks good as well as tastes good. 1 roaster boneless breast 2 tablespoons curry powder 1/4 teaspoon salt or to taste 1 tablespoon vegetable oil 1 can (20-ounces) pineapple chunks, well drained 1/2 pound (about 60) seedless grapes 60 cocktail toothpicks Yogurt Sauce in Zucchini Cups (recipe follows) Cut breast into 50 to 60 bite-sized chunks. Place chicken chunks in large bowl; add curry powder and salt; toss together. In a large, heavy non-stick skillet over medium heat, heat oil. Add curried chicken chunks; reduce heat to low and saute for 10 minutes, turning to cook all sides. Cover and remove from heat; cool. Thread cooled chicken onto toothpicks with a chunk of pineapple and a grape. Serve with Yogurt Sauce as dip. YOGURT SAUCE IN ZUCCHINI CUPS for Curried Chicken and Fruit Kebabs 1 container (16-ounces) plain yogurt 3 tablespoons honey 2 tablespoons minced fresh coriander (also called cilantro or Chinese parsley) or 1/2 teaspoon ground coriander seed 1 teaspoon ground ginger 1 tablespoon fresh lemon juice 4 or 5 medium-sized zucchini, optional In medium-sized bowl, combine yogurt, honey, coriander, ginger and lemon juice. If desired, spoon into individual zucchini cups for each guest. To make cups, cut each zucchini crosswise into 6 equal pieces. Use a melon baller to scoop out centers from one end of each piece.

ORIENTAL MINI DRUMSTICKSMakes about 54 If the honey you're planning on using for this recipe has been around awhile and crystallized, you can re-liquify it by heating the opened jar gently in hot water. You can do the same thing in the microwave, but do it at low power and take the honey out as soon as it's become liquid again. Don't heat the honey for longer than it takes to re- liquify; you would lose some of the delicate flavor. 30 chicken wings 1 bottle (5-ounces) teriyaki sauce 1/4 cup peanut or vegetable oil 1/4 cup honey 1 tablespoon white vinegar 1 teaspoon ground ginger 2 cups lightly toasted, finely-chopped peanuts or pecans With sharp, kitchen knife, divide wings into three sections, cutting between joints — not bone. Reserve first and middle joints for mini drumsticks; set wing tips aside for stock or another use. To make mini drums from the first joint: Using a small sharp knife, cut around the narrower end to loosen meat.

Then, use knife blade to gently scrape meat down toward the larger, knobby end of bone, turning meat inside out. To make mini drums from middle joints: Cut around the narrower end; cut tendons away and loosen meat. Then use knife blade to gently scrape meat along both bones toward the larger end. Pull out smaller bone, detaching with knife if necessary. Turn meat inside out around knob of remaining bone. In large bowl, combine teriyaki sauce, oil, honey, vinegar and ginger; mix well. Add chicken and coat well. Cover and marinate overnight in refrigerator. Preheat oven to 3250F. Grease 2 large baking sheets with sides; arrange chicken on baking sheets. Bake for 35 minutes or until cooked through. Remove and roll in chopped nuts. Serve hot or at room temperature.

SANTA FE CHICKEN QUESADILLAS (Kay sa diyas)Makes about 64 If you want to make this way ahead of time, you can cool and then freeze the ungarnished quesadilla wedges between layers of aluminum foil. Reheat in preheated 3000F oven for 20 minutes and then add the garnish. 4 roaster boneless thigh cutlets 2 cloves garlic 2 teaspoons ground cumin 1 teaspoon salt or to taste 1/4 teaspoon ground pepper 2 tablespoons vegetable oil 2 cans (4-ounces each) chopped mild green chilies 1 minced, canned or fresh Jalapeno pepper (optional) 16 flour tortillas (8 inches each) 8 tablespoons minced fresh coriander (also called cilantro or Chinese parsley), optional 1 pound Monterey Jack or Cheddar cheese, grated Mexican salsa or slivers of avocado sprinkled with lemon juice, chopped tomato, and coriander sprigs Cut each thigh into 4 pieces. In container of food processor fitted with steel blade, finely mince garlic. Gradually add chicken pieces, cumin, salt and pepper; grind to a fine texture. In a large heavy, non-stick skillet, heat oil. Add ground chicken mixture and cook over medium heat, stirring often. Cook for 8 to 10 minutes or until meat is no longer pink. Preheat oven to 3000F. Drain chilies and add to cooked chicken. Place 8 tortillas on 2 large baking sheets and brush lightly with water. Divide chicken mixture among the 8 tortillas, spreading a thin layer almost to the edges. Sprinkle with chopped coriander and grated cheese; top with remaining tortillas, pressing down edges to seal. Brush lightly with water and bake for 15 minutes. Remove from oven and cut each quesadilla into 8 wedges. If desired, serve with Mexican salsa or top with avocado, tomato and coriander. SHERRY FRIED CHICKEN LIVERS Makes 12 I know people who didn't think they could lik think they could like chicken livers who are won over when the flavor of sherry wine is added. 12 chicken livers (about 1 lb.) 2 tablespoons butter or margarine 1 1/2 teaspoons salt or to taste 1/4 teaspoon ground pepper 1/2 cup dry sherry In a large skillet over medium heat, melt butter. Add chicken livers and saute for 6 to 8 minutes. Sprinkle with salt and pepper. Add sherry, cover, and simmer 5 minutes longer or until cooked through. Serve on toothpicks.

BLUE CHEESE CHICKEN SPREADMakes about 40 Although I usually prefer fresh products to canned ones, in this case I recommend using canned pineapple. Fresh pineapple has an unusual characteristic that's worth knowing. It contains the enzyme bromelin which breaks down protein. The blue cheese in this recipe is rich in protein and fresh pineapple would not work well with it, unless you added it just before serving so the bromelin doesn't have a chance to break down the proteins and give it an off- flavor. Canned pineapple, on the other hand, doesn't have enough active bromelin to cause a problem. Makes approx. 40 party sandwiches (1 tablespoon per sandwich) 1 cup cooked, ground chicken 1 jar (5 oz.) blue cheese spread 1/2 cup drained, crushed pineapple 1/2 cup chopped almonds, lightly toasted Salt and ground pepper to taste In a bowl combine chicken with remaining ingredients. Use as filling for party sandwiches. MAIN COURSES - 7 CHICKEN CORDON BLEU FOR A CROWD Serves 15-20 There are many recipes for Chicken Cordon Bleu, but I like this one because you can do everything the day before. Reheat it in the microwave. Don't, however, freeze it. Fried foods tend to get a "warmed over" taste after freezing. Also, don't hold it in the refrigerator for longer than a day.

And finally, when reheating it in the microwave, be sure to rotate it several times so that you don't have uneven warming. (Rotating the food in the oven performs the same function as stirring a pot. If you don't rotate it, you risk having some parts overcooked$and overcooked chicken is tough chicken.) 20 boneless, skinless chicken breast halves 1 cup butter or margarine, melted 1/3 cup minced, fresh parsley 20 slices Canadian bacon or ham 20 slices sharp or Swiss cheese 3 eggs, beaten 2 cups bread crumbs Slice each breast half almost in half lengthwise and then open like the wings of a butterfly. Brush with melted butter and sprinkle with parsley. Place slice of bacon or ham and slice of cheese on each chicken breast, folding to fit. Roll, jelly-roll fashion, and secure with toothpicks. Dip in beaten eggs and roll in bread crumbs. Fry in deep fat at 350oF for 12 to 15 minutes or until golden brown and cooked through.. Remove toothpicks before serving. Keep warm in a preheated 325oF if serving within 30 minutes or reheat in a preheated 350oF for 10 to 15 minutes. CHICKEN SALAD HAWAIIANServes 12-15 This recipe is good for a summer lunch. You should keep it cold until serving, but contrary to popular belief, mayonnaise itself isn't particularly dangerous from a food safety point of view. Mayonnaise in its usual commercial formulations is acid enough to be mildly protective against harmful microorganisms. But it's not protective enough, so don't take chances and do keep this refrigerated until you need it. 6 cups cooked chicken, cut in chunks 1-1/2 cups mayonnaise or salad dressing 2 cups chopped celery 2 tablespoons soy sauce 1 can (#2 size or 2 1/2 cups) pineapple tidbits, drained 1/2 cup slivered almonds, lightly toasted, divided In a large mixing bowl combine chicken, mayonnaise, celery and soy sauce. Gently fold in pineapple and half of almond slivers. Serve salad on a platter lined with lettuce leaves. Garnish with remaining almonds. CREAMED CHICKEN VICTORIAServes 10-12 This is a good buffet dish because your guests don't have to cut anything while balancing their dinner plates on their laps. I've expanded it to feed as many as 60 people, and it always draws raves. As an additional bonus, it's at least as good the next day for leftovers. You may find, as I have, that it's easier to add the flour right after sauteing the mushrooms and skip sauteing the chicken. You can also use leftover chicken and skip cooking the roaster breasts; I've done it and it works just fine. The original recipe called for twice as much mustard. If you like your foods quite spicy, you may want to use the four teaspoons of mustard that the original recipe called for. 2 whole roaster breasts, 2-1/2 to 3 pounds each 8 cups chicken broth 1/2 cup butter or margarine 1 pound fresh mushrooms, sliced 1/2 cup flour 2 teaspoons dry mustard salt to taste, depending on saltiness of the broth 1/2 teaspoon Cayenne pepper or to taste 2 cups light cream or half and half 1 cup dry sherry 1/4 cup grated Parmesan cheese 1/4 cup minced fresh parsley Puffed Pastry Hearts (recipe follows) or toast points In 4-quart Dutch oven or large, deep skillet over high heat, bring chicken broth to a boil. Add roaster breasts and enough water to cover, if necessary. Reduce heat to low; simmer for 70 minutes. Cool breasts in broth. Remove and cut into 1/2-inch dice; discard bones and skin. Reserve 2 cups broth for recipe; save remainder for another use. In same Dutch oven or skillet over medium-high heat, melt butter; add mushrooms and saute 30 seconds. Add diced chicken and saute 30 seconds longer. Stir in flour, seasonings, 2 cups reserved broth and cream; bring to a simmer. Reduce heat to low and simmer 5 minutes, stirring frequently. Add sherry, Parmesan cheese and parsley. Simmer 1 minute longer. Serve chicken with Puff Pastry Hearts or toast points. PUFF PASTRY HEARTS to go with Chicken Victoria You can bake the Puff Pastry Hearts 1 or 2 days in advance. Store thoroughly-cooled hearts in an airtight container. 1 package (17-1/2-ounces) frozen puff pastry 1 3-inch heart-shaped cookie cutter 1 whole egg beaten with 1 tablespoon water Defrost pastry 20 minutes at room temperature. Preheat oven to 375F. Open one sheet at a time onto a lightly- floured board. Cut hearts from pastry and place on two dampened cookie sheets. Pierce hearts with tines of a fork.

Then, using the back of a small knife, decorate tops and edges. Brush tops lightly with egg wash. Bake 20 minutes or until golden.

CURRIED CHICKEN RAJ Serves 10-12 This is another dish that works well for a buffet. It's easy to serve and easy to eat since the guests don't need to cut anything. 2 whole roaster breasts 2 and 1/2 to 3 pounds each 1/2 cup butter or margarine 8 cups chicken broth 3/4 cup raisins 1/4 cup curry powder 1/2 cup flour 1-1/4 teaspoons salt or to taste 1/4 teaspoon Cayenne pepper or to taste 1/4 teaspoon ground pepper 2 cups light cream or half and half 1/4 cup minced fresh parsley Puffed Pastry Hearts (see recipe) or toast points Chutney, slivered toasted almonds, other condiments, optional In 4-quart Dutch oven or large, deep skillet over high heat, bring chicken broth to a boil. Add roaster breasts and enough water to cover, if necessary. Reduce heat to low; simmer chicken for 70 minutes. Cool chicken in broth. Remove meat and cut into 1/2-inch cubes; discard skin and bones. Reserve 3 cups broth for recipe; save remainder for another use. In same Dutch oven or skillet over medium-high heat, melt butter, stir in chicken, raisins, and curry powder; saute for 1 minute. Stir in flour, seasonings, reserved 3 cups broth, and cream; bring to a simmer. Reduce heat to low and simmer 5 minutes, stirring frequently. Stir in parsley. Serve chicken with Puff Pastry Hearts or toast points, accompanied by chutney, toasted almonds, or other condiments, if desired.

JUST PLAIN BARBECUED CHICKEN Serves 50 If you visit the Delmarva Peninsula (Delaware, Maryland, Virginia) in summer, you may come across some of the chicken barbecues that take place here. This is one of the popular recipes for crowds. 50 chicken breast halves 25 drumsticks 2 quarts oil 2 quarts vinegar 8 tablespoons salt or to taste 3 tablespoons ground pepper In a 2 gallon container, combine oil, vinegar, salt and pepper. Grill chicken 5 to 6 inches above medium-hot coals for 20 to 30 minutes or until cooked through. Turn and brush with sauce every 10 to 15 minutes.

SWEET 'N SMOKEY CHICKEN Serves 30-40 My step daughter-in-law, Jan Perdue, says that when Frank's son Jim was courting her, he invited her over for dinner and served Sweet 'n Smokey Chicken for two. Jan was enchanted with his culinary skill and thought that this would be a sample of what marriage to him would be like. She learned later that this is just about the only thing he cooks. Fortunately, she enjoys cooking and doesn't mind. 30 chicken breast halves 15 chicken drumsticks 15 chicken thighs 8 medium onions, sliced 2 quarts ketchup 1 cup prepared mustard 2 cups vinegar 1 quart maple syrup 1/4 cup hickory smoked salt or to taste 2 teaspoons ground pepper Preheat oven to 350oF. Place chicken in a single layer, skin side up on top of onion slices in the bottom of 2 to 3 large baking pans. If possible keep breast halves in a separate pan from legs and thighs as they will cook more quickly. In a 2 gallon container combine remaining ingredients and pour over chicken. Bake chicken, uncovered for 45 to 60 minutes or until cooked through. Check breast meat for doneness after 45 minutes.

TREASURE ISLAND CHICKENServes 30-40 A school-lunch chicken recipe contest produced this one. The winner adapted it from an old family recipe. 30 chicken breast halves 15 chicken drumsticks 15 chicken thighs 1/2 pound butter or margarine 1/2 cup flour 3/4 cup sugar 1 teaspoon dry mustard 2 teaspoons cinnamon 1/2 teaspoon ground ginger 1 quart orange juice 2 tablespoons salt or to taste Preheat oven to 350oF. Place chicken in single layer, skin side up, in 2 to 3 large baking pans. Keep breast halves in a separate pan as they will cook more quickly than the legs and thighs. In a large saucepan over medium heat, melt butter. Stir in flour, sugar, spices, orange juice and salt and cook, stirring constantly until thickened. Pour sauce over chicken. Bake, uncovered, for 45 to 60 minutes or until cooked through. Check breast meat for doneness after 45 minutes. TEXAS BARBECUED BREASTSServes 10-16 Turn chicken breasts with tongs instead of a fork, which could pierce the meat and cause it to lose some of its juiciness. 1 cup tomato sauce 1/4 cup red wine vinegar 1/4 cup chili sauce 1/4 cup brown sugar 3 tablespoons grated onion 2 tablespoons Worcestershire sauce 1 tablespoon Dijon mustard 1/2 teaspoon chili powder 1 teaspoon paprika 1/2 teaspoon Tabasco (optional) 16 chicken breast halves In a large saucepan over medium heat combine all ingredients except chicken and bring to a boil. Grill chicken 5 to 6 inches above medium-hot coals for 25 to 30 minutes or until cooked through. Turn and baste 3 to 4 times with sauce during cooking.

CHAPTER SEVEN$ CHICKEN FOR TOMORROW$OR NEXT WEEK.

In an ideal world, we'd always have food at its freshest and we'd eat it right after it was prepared. In the real world, though, there are many, many times when cooking ahead is useful. You're giving a party and you don't want to be frazzled the day of the event. Or you've got a busy week coming up and you want to do better by your family than just giving them calorie-laden, greasy take-out food. Or you're having house guests, and you want to spend the time with them instead of in the kitchen. Or maybe there's only one or two of you at home, and you've discovered that it's simpler to make a recipe for four and freeze part of it for use later.

In my own case, my freezer is always full. One reason is that Frank often invites three or four people the last minute, and it helps to have emergency food on hand. Equally often, after I've made a meal, he'll call at 6:00 p.m. and tell me that we're eating out with one of the poultry distributors or suppliers, and I end up freezing what I've just cooked. As I wrap the food in foil and wedge it into the freezer, I remind myself, "This meal isn't going to waste, it's a head start on a future meal."

When you know the principles for successful freezing$and I'll get to them in a moment$you can freeze just about any of the recipes in this cookbook. The recipes in this chapter are different from the rest because they not only can be cooked ahead, often they should be cooked ahead. Some of them require marination, others improve with age, and still others adapt so well to cooking the day before that they belong in this chapter. Use this chapter for recipes to use when you want to cook a day or so ahead of time, and also, use it for tips on how to freeze foods successfully.

There are just a few principles needed to master the technique of cooking ahead, and once you know them, you'll have faster, better-tasting, healthier and safer meals to show for it.

_The biggest boon to food preparation ahead is the freezer. Everything freezes from the point of view of food safety, but there's a lot of variation in palatability. For best flavor and texture, don't freeze the following foods in your home freezer:

- Milk products — they'll curdle.

- Boiled eggs — the whites get watery.

- Custards — they'll lose texture, get lumpy.

- Mayonnaise — it may separate.

- Most foods that you fry at home (except french fries and onions) — they can get an unattractive "warmed-over" taste. It's actually the fats turning slightly rancid.

- Cooked potatoes — they darken and get an unattractive texture. (If you're going to freeze stew, add cooked potatoes later on when you're reheating the stew.)

- Fresh greens, celery, and carrots — they get limp.

- Fresh tomatoes — their high water content causes them to collapse when thawed. (However, you can freeze tomatoes if you're going to use them in a cooked form, such as in a pasta sauce.)

- Gravy — the fat will separate out and puddle. (If you must freeze gravy, cut way back on the fat when you're making the gravy, and stir constantly when you're reheating it so as to keep the fat from separating.)

- Heavily spiced foods — most herbs, salts, onions, fade away, but garlic and cloves will seem more intense. Pepper has a tendency to turn bitter. Curry takes on a musty flavor.

- Synthetic flavors — use real vanilla rather than synthetic because synthetic vanilla can have an off-flavor after freezing.

_Highly salted foods $ salt tends to attract moisture and uneven freezing may result because salt slows down the freezing process.

_Even if you're freezing food for only a couple of days, be careful of packaging. Air that's in the package will affect the color, flavor and texture. The container should be air tight, or the food will get freezer burn and lose nutritional value, and palatability.

_It's critical to have a both your refrigerator and freezer cold enough. The best indicator of a good freezer temperature is brick-hard ice cream. If ice cream stored in your freezer is soft, turn the control to a colder setting. As for the refrigerator, check the drinking temperature of milk. If it's very cold, you've probably hit 40 degrees, which is what you're aiming for. If the milk isn't cold enough, or if it sours too quickly, move the control to a colder setting.

_Here's a great tip if you're freezing chicken in a polyethylene bag: lower the bag, with the chicken in it, into a pan of water to force out the air. Be sure the bag opening is above water. Press entire surface area of bag to squeeze out air bubbles. Twist end of bag and fold over. Secure with fastener and label.

_Here's a convenient way to freeze casseroles for later use that Joy Schrage from Whirlpool Corporation told me:

       1. Line the casserole dish with foil, leaving 2" collar all around.

2. Add casserole ingredients and bake.

3. Cool and freeze in uncovered casserole

4. When frozen, lift casserole and foil out in one piece

5. Cover with foil or place in a polyethylene freezer bag. Press air out, then seal tightly, label, date and freeze. Place in a polyethylene freezer bag.

6. To thaw, take frozen casserole out of bag and foil, and place in the casserole dish it was originally baked in.

This type of freezing frees the casserole dish for other uses while the casserole is in the freezer.

_Homemade "TV" dinners: Place leftovers in serving portions on sectioned plastic trays. Cover, chill, tightly with plastic wrap and seal. Then wrap entire tray in foil. Label, date and freeze. To reheat, remove foil, puncture plastic wrap to make steam vents, and heat dinner in microwave.

_To keep chicken pieces from sticking together in your freezer so that you can take out just the quantity you want without prying several pieces apart or thawing more than you need, do the following:

1. Spread pieces in a single layer on a cookie sheet

2. Place unwrapped in freezer

3. Once frozen, remove chicken pieces from cookie sheet, and store in polyethylene freezer bag

5. Place bag in freezer, label and date

_Freezing tip - use freezing tape to seal freezer wrap or suitable plastic wrap. Freezer tape is made with a special adhesive designed to stick at low temperatures.

_Whole birds to be roasted should be thawed before cooking. Broilers, and birds to be cooked by other methods can start being cooked when thawed enough for pieces to separate.

If you'll follow the suggestions above, you'll find that most of the foods you cook can be prepared ahead of time and if necessary, frozen. This means that, with the exception of fried foods, just about all the recipes in this book can be considered cook-ahead foods.

So, whether you're cooking for a party, for the week's meals, for houseguests, or for yourself, enjoy the recipes that follow$and all the others in this book as well. CRISPY CORNISH A LA BLEUServes 2 There are easily 50 varieties of blue vein cheeses for sale in this country. Probably the most famous are the French Roqueforta, the Italian Gorgonzola, the English Stilton, and the American Treasure Cavea. Personally, I like the American varieties best. 2 fresh Cornish game hens Oil for deep frying 1/2 cup mayonnaise 1/4 cup sour cream 1/4 cup minced onion 1/4 cup crumbled bleu cheese 1 small clove garlic, minced Celery sticks Cut hens into 8 pieces each. Fry in deep hot oil at 375F, turning once, until golden brown on both sides, about ten minutes. Drain well on paper towels. Refrigerate if not serving right away. In a small bowl combine remaining ingredients except celery. Cover and chill. Serve hens warm, at room temperature or cold with bleu cheese dip and celery sticks. CHICKEN SOUFFLEServes 4 This is a nice prepare-ahead item. It's really best if stored overnight in the refrigerator before baking so the flavors have a chance to blend. 4 eggs, beaten 1 teaspoon minced, fresh thyme or 1/4 teaspoon dried 1 teaspoon minced, fresh basil or 1/4 teaspoon dried Ground pepper to taste 2 cups cooked, shredded chicken 1/4 pound ham, roughly chopped 1 tablespoon minced, fresh parsley 1/2 cup grated Parmesan cheese, divided 3 cups chicken broth 1/2 loaf (5 ounces) Italian bread, roughly torn into chunks 1 cup grated mozzarella cheese In a mixing bowl combine eggs, thyme, basil and pepper. Add chicken, ham, parsley, 1/4 cup Parmesan cheese and broth. Combine thoroughly and set aside. Butter an 8" x 12" baking dish. Place bread chunks in the bottom. Cover with egg mixture followed by Mozzarella cheese and remaining Parmesan. Refrigerate 1 hour or longer. Preheat oven to 350oF. Bake for 45 minutes until puffed and golden brown.

CHICKEN AND STUFFING Serves 6 I wouldn't serve this to a gourmet club, but it's an easy, cook ahead dish for a relaxed family meal when you don't want to spend a lot of time in the kitchen. It's also an ideal way to have the taste of stuffed chicken — with easier serving qualities. You can make it ahead of time, up to the point of baking. 2 cans (10-1/2-ounces each) condensed cream of chicken soup, divided 1 can (10-1/2-ounces) chicken broth 2 eggs, beaten 1 package (7-1/2-ounces) herb seasoned stuffing mix 3 cups cooked chicken, cut in chunks 1 teaspoon salt or to taste 1/8 teaspoon ground pepper 1/2 cup milk 2 tablespoons chopped canned pimento Preheat oven to 350oF. In a mixing bowl whisk together one can of undiluted soup, broth and eggs. Add stuffing mix and toss. Place stuffing in bottom of a baking dish. Arrange chicken on top of stuffing and sprinkle with salt and pepper. In a large measuring cup combine remaining can of soup and milk and pimento and pour over all. Bake, uncovered, for 35 to 45 minutes or until hot and bubbling..

CHICK-O-TATO CASSEROLE Serves 4-6 This tastes better reheated, after the flavors have had a chance to blend. You can make it today and it will taste better tomorrow. 1/3 cup vegetable oil 1/2 cup chopped onion 1/2 cup chopped celery 1/2 cup chopped green pepper 1/2 cup ketchup 1/2 cup water 2 tablespoons vinegar 2 tablespoons sugar 1 tablespoon Worcestershire sauce 1 tablespoon prepared mustard 1 teaspoon salt or to taste 1/4 teaspoon ground pepper 1 chicken, cut in serving pieces 4 medium potatoes, peeled and thickly sliced Preheat oven to 350F. In a large skillet, over medium heat, heat oil. Add onion, celery and green pepper and cook, stirring often, for 6 to 8 minutes or until softened. Add ketchup, water, vinegar, sugar, Worcestershire sauce, mustard, salt and pepper and simmer at low heat for about 15 minutes. Place chicken in bottom of a baking dish and tuck potatoes around chicken pieces. Pour sauce over all. Bake, covered, for 50 to 60 minutes or until cooked through. If planning to reheat, remove from oven when slightly under cooked. CHOICE CHEESY CHICKEN Serves 4-6 There's no last minute attention required for this recipe. Prepare it a day ahead, right up to the point of baking. 1 clove garlic, peeled 1/2 cup (1 stick) butter or margarine 1 cup bread crumbs 1/2 cup grated sharp Cheddar cheese 1/4 cup grated Parmesan cheese 1 teaspoon salt or to taste 1/8 teaspoon ground pepper 6 skinless, boneless chicken breast halves With the broad side of a large kitchen knife crush garlic slightly to release flavor. In a small saucepan over low heat melt butter with garlic clove. Set butter aside for 1/2 hour for maximum garlic flavoring. On a sheet of wax paper combine bread crumbs, cheeses, salt and pepper. Dip chicken in garlic butter, then roll in cheese mixture. Tuck sides under to form a neat roll. Arrange chicken in a large shallow baking pan and drizzle with any remaining butter. Cover and refrigerate if making ahead. When ready to bake, preheat oven to 350oF. Bake chicken for 35 to 45 minutes or until crisp, golden and cooked through. PHOTO: New Year's Eve - Cold "Chicken Tonnato" Buffet

COLD CHICKEN TONNATOServes 6-8 This is an elegant company recipe, and it works well if you make it the day before. I've made it with water-packed tuna, but oil-packed would work also. 8 chicken cutlets (about 2 pounds skinless, boneless chicken breast halves, pounded thin, or 2 thin sliced boneless roaster breasts) 1/2 cup flour, seasoned with salt and ground pepper to taste 1/2 cup (1 stick) butter or margarine 2 cans (13-ounces) tuna, drained 8 anchovies 2 cloves garlic, peeled 1 cup olive oil 4 tablespoons white vinegar 4 tablespoons light cream 2 tablespoons capers Dip cutlets in flour to coat lightly, shake off excess. In a large skillet over medium-high heat, melt butter. Add cutlets and saute until cooked through, about 5 minutes; turn once. Drain cutlets on paper towels. Chill. In a blender or food processor, combine tuna, anchovies, garlic, oil, vinegar and light cream. Blend until pureed. Pour sauce over cold cutlets, sprinkle with capers. May be loosely covered and refrigerated overnight before serving.

EASY CHICKEN CORDON BLEUServes 4 This is another recipe that can be fixed, except for frying, on the day before. For variation, try Swiss cheese and Canadian bacon. For a sauce, make a white sauce with chicken broth. If you're in a hurry, undiluted cream of chicken soup makes a handy substitute, but it's definitely a second choice compared to a good, homemade white sauce. Garnish with parsley sprig. 4 skinless, boneless chicken breast halves or 1 thin sliced boneless roaster breast 4 tablespoons butter or margarine 1 tablespoon minced, fresh parsley 4 slices ham 4 slices sharp cheese 1 egg, beaten 1 cup bread crumbs Place chicken between sheets of plastic wrap and pound to 1/4 inch thickness. Skip the preceding step if you're using the thin sliced boneless roaster breast. Spread chicken with butter and sprinkle with parsley. Place a slice of ham and a slice of cheese on each chicken breast, folding to fit. Roll, jelly-roll fashion, and secure with toothpicks. Dip chicken in beaten egg and roll in bread crumbs. Fry in deep fat at 350oF for 12-15 minutes or until golden brown and cooked through. Remove toothpicks before serving.

FIESTA TORTILLA STACK 6-8 servings The flavors in this recipe blend and get better if you make it the day before, but I have also served it the same day when I was in a hurry. It does need at least a couple of hours for the flavors to develop. I've made this recipe with coriander and without; it works well either way. Coriander, by the way, is also known as cilantro or Chinese parsley, so if you can't find "coriander" in your market, look for it by its other names. 1 cup cooked, shredded chicken 1/2 cup mayonnaise 3 tablespoons chopped, fresh, cilantro (also called coriander or Chinese parsley), if available 1/2 teaspoon salt 1 package (8 ounces) cream cheese 1 can (7 ounces) whole kernel corn, drained 2 tablespoons taco seasoning mix 1 dozen 8-inch flour tortillas Cherry tomatoes 1 small head lettuce In a mixing bowl combine chicken, mayonnaise, cilantro and salt. In a separate small bowl combine cream cheese drained corn and taco seasoning mix. Place 2 flour tortillas, one on top of other. Spread with 1/3 of chicken mixture, then two tortillas and corn mixture. Continue until mixtures are used up. Chill for at least 4 hours to develop flavors. Remove from refrigerator half an hour before serving. Garnish with tomatoes and serve on a bed of lettuce.

GARDEN BREAST CHEVREServes 4 Chevre means goat in French, and the title of this recipe comes from the goat cheese in it. Frank, by the way, loves goat cheese. 1 whole roaster breast salt and ground pepper to taste 6 ounces mild creamy goat cheese or cream cheese, softened 1 medium carrot, coarsely grated 1 small zucchini, unpeeled and coarsely grated 1/4 cup snipped fresh or frozen chives 2 teaspoons minced fresh rosemary or 1/2 teaspoon dried 1 tablespoon vegetable oil Preheat oven to 375o F. Working from the top of the breast use finger tips to carefully loosen the skin from the meat on the breast to form a pocket. Do not detach skin on sides or at base of breast.. Combine cheese, carrot, zucchini, chives, rosemary and salt and pepper. Stuff vegetable mixture evenly under skin of breast. Brush with oil and place skin side up in a roasting pan. Bake for about one hour and 15 minutes or until juices run clear with no hint of pink when a cut is made near the bone. Chill, wrap tightly and refrigerate if not serving immediately. It's good served at room temperature, but it's also good reheated.

COLD CORNISHServes 2 To get the best flavor from the green beans in this recipe, choose ones that are fresh and young. The bean growers say that if the bean is fresh, it will snap easily when broken. If it bends instead of snapping, the bean has been around too long. Also, check the maturity of the developing seeds inside the pods. You want the seeds to be immature, and you can tell this by making sure that they don't bulge inside the pods. If the seeds are bulging, you can count on the green beans being tough and leathery. 2 fresh Cornish game hens 2 tablespoons olive oil 2 large tomatoes, coarsely chopped, or 1 can (16 ounces) whole tomatoes, chopped, drained 1 medium zucchini, sliced 1 cup fresh green beans, cut into 2-inch lengths 4 scallions, sliced 1/4 cup minced fresh basil or 1 tablespoon dried 1 teaspoon salt or to taste 1/8 teaspoon ground pepper 1 cup chicken broth 1/3 cup Feta cheese (optional) Quarter hens, remove backbones. In a large skillet, over medium-high heat, heat oil. Add hens and brown on all sides, 12 to 15 minutes. Add remaining ingredients. Cover and simmer 20 minutes or until hens are cooked through. Refrigerate. Serve cold, sprinkled with cheese.

KICK-OFF KABOBSServes 6 Frank is an avid sports fan, and he constantly astonishes his friends by knowing obscure facts and dates concerning the various players and games. This is a an easy dish to serve your sports fans. 6 skinless, boneless chicken breast halves 1/4 cup flour 1 teaspoon salt or to taste 1/8 teaspoon ground pepper 1 egg, slightly beaten 2 tablespoons water 1/2 cup fine dry bread crumbs 1/4 cup grated Parmesan cheese 3 tablespoons butter or margarine Preheat oven to 375oF. On a sheet of wax paper, combine flour, salt and pepper. In a shallow dish beat together egg and water. On a separate sheet of wax paper blend bread crumbs and cheese. Dip chicken into flour, then egg, then bread crumb mixture turning to coat well on both sides. Arrange chicken in a buttered baking dish. Dot with remaining butter. Bake for 15 minutes. Turn and bake 15 to 20 minutes longer or until cooked through. Cut each breast half into four pieces and thread onto wooden skewers. Wrap in foil or place in plastic container and refrigerate until needed. Serve with assorted dips. Herbed Sour Cream Dip - In a small bowl combine 1 cup sour cream, 3 tablespoons minced fresh parsley, 1 teaspoon dried tarragon, 2 tablespoons minced scallions, 2 tablespoons snipped fresh or frozen chives, and 1/2 teaspoon salt or to taste. Instant Spiced Dip - In a small bowl blend together 1 cup mayonnaise, 1/4 cup bottled French dressing, 1/4 cup chili sauce, 1 teaspoon horseradish sauce, 1 teaspoon Worcestershire sauce, 1/2 teaspoon dry mustard, 2 cloves garlic, minced and salt to taste. (If you're in a hurry, substitute 1/2 teaspoon garlic salt for the fresh garlic and the salt.)

MARINATED BROILED CHICKEN Serves 2-4 Marinating provides an opportunity for flavors to penetrate the chicken. The marinating time can vary tremendously and the results will still be tasty. I like to marinate overnight, in the refrigerator, but even three hours can add a lot to the flavor or your chicken. 1 chicken, cut in half lengthwise 1/2 cup peanut or vegetable oil 1/2 cup soy sauce 1 teaspoon minced, fresh ginger or 1 teaspoon ground 2 cloves garlic, minced Salt to taste Place chicken in a shallow dish. Add remaining ingredients and turn to coat well. Cover and marinate refrigerated for at least 3 hours. Place chicken skin side down on broiler rack. Pour half of marinade mixture in cavity of chicken. Broil 9 to 10 inches from broiler for about 30 minutes. Turn chicken, brush with remaining mixture. Broil 20 to 30 minutes longer or until cooked through.

OVEN-BRAISED ROASTER BREAST WITH VEGETABLES Serves 4-6 Making this dish the day before has a couple of advantages. Any fat will rise to the top where it's easy to remove and also the wine and herbs "marry" with the other flavors. 1 whole roaster breast 2 tablespoons vegetable oil 8 small white onions (about 1/2 pound) 1-1/2 cups low-sodium chicken broth 1/3 cup dry white wine 1 tablespoon minced, fresh tarragon or 1 teaspoon dried 1/4 teaspoon ground pepper 8 small potatoes, peeled 8 baby carrots 2 cups broccoli florets 1/4 cup milk 1-1/2 tablespoons cornstarch Preheat oven to 350oF. In 5-quart oven-proof Dutch oven or saucepot over medium-high heat, heat oil. Add roaster breast; cook 15 to 20 minutes turning until browned on all sides. Remove and set aside. Add onions, cook 2 to 3 minutes or until lightly browned, stirring frequently. Remove onions; pour off excess fat. Return roaster breast to Dutch oven. Add broth, wine, tarragon and pepper; bring to a boil. Add potatoes; cover and bake 30 minutes. Add onions and carrots; cover. Bake 30 minutes longer or until roaster breast and vegetables are almost tender. Add broccoli; cover. Bake 8 to 10 minutes longer or until roaster breast is cooked through and vegetables are tender. (Prepare to this point and refrigerate overnight, if desired.) Remove roaster breast and vegetables to serving platter; keep warm. In small bowl, stir together milk and cornstarch until smooth; stir into liquid in Dutch oven. Over medium heat, bring to boil; boil 1 minute, stirring constantly. Serve sauce with roaster breast and vegetables.

PARMESAN BREASTServes 4 Parmesan cheese is a "cooking cheese" and is usually used in its grated form in the United States. When young, it's mild and nutty, but with age is acquires a sharply tangy flavor. When it's too old, it gives an off-flavor to foods, so check the shelf life on the container. When it doubt, taste it. 1 whole roaster breast 2 cups cooked rice 1 cup fresh chopped spinach (or 1/2 package frozen, thawed and drained) 1/2 cup minced fresh basil, or 2 tablespoons dried 1 clove garlic, minced 1/4 cup toasted pine nuts 1 egg 2 tablespoons milk 2 tablespoons olive oil, plus 1 tablespoon for basting 1/4 cup grated Parmesan cheese Salt and ground pepper to taste Preheat oven to 375oF. Season breast to taste with salt and pepper. In a mixing bowl combine remaining ingredients. Stuff breast cavity with rice and place a sheet of aluminum foil over cavity to hold in stuffing. Carefully turn breast over and place skin side up in a roasting pan. Spoon any remaining rice around breast. Baste chicken with oil and bake for about one hour and 30 minutes or until juices run clear with no hint of pink when a cut is made near the bone. Chill, wrap tightly, and refrigerate for 24 hours to give flavors a chance to blend. You can serve it warm or at room temperature.

SALISBURY CHICKEN BREASTS

Serves 6-8

The name "Salisbury," when used with steak means that the beef will be chopped or ground. This recipe has nothing to do with chopped meat; in this case "Salisbury" refers to the town on Maryland's Eastern Shore where the Perdue Farms headquarters is located. You can prepare this a day ahead of time right up to the point of baking.

8 skinless, boneless chicken breast halves or two thin sliced boneless roaster breasts
1/2 cup flour
1-1/2 teaspoons salt or to taste
1/4 teaspoon ground pepper
1 cup bread crumbs
3/4 teaspoon minced, fresh sage or 1/4 teaspoon dried
3/4 teaspoon minced, fresh rosemary or 1/4 teaspoon dried
3/4 teaspoon minced, fresh thyme or 1/4 teaspoon dried
2 eggs
1/2 cup (1 stick) butter or margarine, melted
1/2 cup Sauterne wine
8 slices mozzarella cheese

Preheat oven to 350oF. On a sheet of wax paper, combine flour, salt and pepper. In a shallow bowl beat eggs. On a separate sheet of wax paper combine bread crumbs and seasonings. Dip chicken in flour mixture, then eggs, then crumb mixture. Roll and secure with toothpicks. Place in large shallow baking pan. Pour melted butter over chicken. Cover and bake for 20 minutes. Remove cover. Pour Sauterne over chicken. Bake, uncovered, 30 minutes more. Fold slices of cheese in half; place one on top of each roll for last 3 minutes or until cheese is melted.

SECRETARIES' SALAD

Serves 15-25

Perdue home economists developed most of the recipes in this book, but this recipe is one of the few that is mine. I served it first at what Frank and I jokingly call the "Perdue High Holiday," National Secretaries' Day. That's the day when we honor the people who we know really make the world go 'round. We usually have about 25 of the top secretaries from Perdue Headquarters for dinner along with their husbands to celebrate the day.

1 head lettuce, shredded
1 cup chopped celery
1 large green, red, or yellow pepper, chopped
1 cup thinly sliced carrots or if it's summer, 1 cup chopped tomato
1 cup chopped scallions
1 cup frozen peas, room temperature, not cooked
1 1/2 cups

mayonnaise (I use Hellmann's) 2 cups cooked, shredded chicken 2-1/2 cups shredded Cheddar cheese In a large glass bowl, layer ingredients in the order given. Refrigerate for 24 hours to develop flavors.

PISTACHIO SMOKED CHICKEN SPREAD The green color and the crunch of the pistachios add a lot to this spread. Be sure to store the pistachios in an airtight container after purchase. Exposure to air affects the texture of the nuts and causes them to become soggy. 1 package cream cheese (8-ounces), room temperature 1 cup finely chopped cooked chicken 1/2 teaspoon salt or to taste 1/8 teaspoon liquid smoke 1/4 chopped pistachios 3 teaspoons fresh lemon juice In a mixing bowl combine ingredients thoroughly. Refrigerate for 24 hours while flavors blend. Serve on crackers, or for a rich and delicious lunch, I have served it on croissants one time and on bagels another day.

SPICY CORNISH HEN TIDBITS Serves 2 This is another of the recipes included in the Perdue Cornish Hen packages that people have requested from Frank dozens and dozens of times over the years. I'm including the recipe exactly as it originally appeared, but you may want to substitute fresh garlic (1 clove), fresh onion (1 tablespoon, finely chopped), and fresh celery (2 tablespoons, finely chopped), for the garlic powder, onion salt, and celery salt. If you make these substitutions, be sure to add salt to taste afterwards. 2 fresh Cornish game hens 1 teaspoon chili powder 1/2 teaspoon garlic powder 1/2 teaspoon onion salt 1/4 teaspoon celery salt 1/4 teaspoon lemon pepper or black pepper 1 cup vegetable oil or as needed 1 cup bottled garlic cheese dressing Cut hens into serving pieces. Combine dry spices and toss hens in spices to coat evenly. Heat oil in large skillet over medium heat and fry Cornish pieces about 8 minutes on each side until tender and golden. Remove and drain on paper towels. Arrange on a serving dish. Cover and refrigerate overnight. To serve, dip Cornish pieces into bottled dressing. Serve at room temperature.